.

Hilltop Scriptural Meditations for Year C Weekend Spiritual Nourishment

Rev. Benjamin A Vima

Order this book online at www.trafford.com
or email orders@trafford.com

Most Trafford titles are also available at major online book retailers.

Print information available on the last page.

ISBN: 978-1-4907-6687-4 (sc)
ISBN: 978-1-4907-6688-1 (e)

Library of Congress Control Number: 2015919227

Trafford rev. 12/03/2015

Trafford PUBLISHING® www.trafford.com

North America & international
toll-free: 1 888 232 4444 (USA & Canada)
fax: 812 355 4082

CONTENTS

DEDICATION

I have performed my preaching ministry in America almost 25 years of which 20 in Tulsa diocese, OK. Indeed there were many criticisms and complaints against my homilies for their lengthiness, strong English accentuation, and speediness. However I persevered in this ministry smilingly due to many wellwishers and kindhearted parishioners who encouraged me by their keen listening and even taking some notes during my homily-deliveries; also after every mass they wished me and expressed their satisfaction over my performances, plus many times offered me their critical inputs to do better. Some among those of my positive critics are Mary Miller, Kenny Longbrake, Joe and Nancy Massaro, Philip and Laura Stizza, Linda Wilson, Chandra Miller, Carolyn Calip, Larry and Cheryl Montanye, and Connie Ringer. It is to them gratefully I dedicate this book.

FOREWORD

Many try to search for God in many places. Jesus's disciples also did the same after his resurrection. But they were told to come up to the "hilltop" to find him. The hilltop is always a favorite place in the Bible for God to show them his power and glory, and to offer them his promises. We read in the Gospels that Jesus used hilltops frequently for his prayer of solitude. Though evangelists don't point out any specific mountains in Palestine, they qualify those places as high mountains, especially when they narrate two important events in Jesus's life: transfiguration and ascension. During all those hilltop moments while Jesus was informed and confirmed by his Father about his true identity and mission, he too shared those inspirations with his followers.

This is how I esteem of my retirement-life of solitude these days. When I am in prayertime, as I have explained in my book *Prayerfully Yours*, I joyfully feel that I am exclusively alone with the Supreme. This means I am spiritually on his hilltop. Physically, the same is true also. My "manufactured home" is situated on a hilltop, though not exactly the Palestinian high mountains. One more attraction to my residence is it is located on a country road named Hilltop Road!

Nevertheless, the primary reason I coined the title of this book is meditating in the presence of God, who is the "Highest." Where the Highest is, there the hilltop is. Abraham Lincoln very beautifully said, "It is not important that God is with us, but rather that we are with God." My hilltop, more than anything else, is my inner sanctuary. I am sure everyone would agree with me; it is easier to climb up the geographical hilltop than to reach to the bottom of the human spirit. The meditations I have written in this work have been collected when I was at his Highest Place. I don't want to fail my readers with a false promise as a typical fraud did in a story.

This cheat invited the villagers to see God appearing on a hilltop on a particular time and day. He collected from them a hundred dollars each and promised that if it was not true, he would give back double the amount of money. When all were at the spot at the right time, the cheat began crying, "I see him. So beautiful!" They all said "Where? Where?" He asked them to concentrate. They did. He asked them to try a little harder. They did but in vain. Finally, the cheat told the desperate crowd, "I am sorry. God tells me he can be seen only by those who have not committed any sin of fornication, adultery, debauchery, murder, or incest during the past seven days." The leader of the village was there. He suddenly shouted, "I see God!" With him, the second person in the village also shouted, "Yes, I see him!" And so all cried out the same. Next day, when those two important men were alone, the second man asked the leader, "Sir, did you really see God?" The leader said, "Hush—actually, I did not. But to keep up my dignity and respect before the public, I had to maintain I was sinless. What about you?" The second man said, "I too did not see God. But since you cried out, I joined with you." And so it was with the crowd!

Let me be very clear. At this favorable "hilltop environment," I began writing these meditations with the same desire of Jesus's disciples to be inspired by becoming more conscious of Jesus's personality and mission; plus, to be closely attached to him and to be sent by him to perform his mission of mercy, forgiveness, justice, truth, joy, and peace. If, by the grace of God, any one of my readers is truly elevated during their meditating with my writing, I would be thanking my Master for such extravagant results. My sole purpose for this book is for all of us—who claim to be disciples of Jesus—to be charmed by and hooked into Jesus's service team of justice and mercy and truth. I wish also, through these meditations, that my readers come to a clear knowledge of salvation. And I pray all of us be granted by the Lord with the blessings Zechariah, father of John the Baptizer, dreamed of *"being rescued from the hand of enemies, without fear we might worship Him in holiness and righteousness before Him all our days"* (Luke 1:74–75).

This book contains fifty-two weekend meditations based on Church Liturgical Year C's Sunday scriptural passages. I dream to see it as a handbook either in the hands of every Christian at his/her Sabbath prayer hours or at the desks of preachers during the preparation of their Sunday homilies.

Wishing all my readers a thrilling hilltop encounter at every weekend . . .

Yours sincerely,
Rev. Benjamin A. Vima

FIRST WEEKEND

First Advent Sunday
Encounter Jesus Not as Stringent
Judge but as Good Shepherd

And then they will see the Son of Man
coming in a cloud with power and great
glory. But when these signs begin to
happen, stand erect and raise your
heads because your redemption is at
hand . . . Beware that your hearts do
not become drowsy from carousing and
drunkenness and the anxieties of daily
life, and that day catch you by surprise
like a trap. For that day will assault
everyone who lives on the face of the
earth. Be vigilant at all times and pray
that you have the strength to escape the
tribulations that are imminent and to
stand before the Son of Man.

(Luke 21:25–36)

By many rituals and customs, like blessing the Advent
wreath and candles, we make the best use of them to show
our longing and hoping for Jesus's coming both in our
hearts and in the daily events—not only this holy season
of beginning the liturgical year, but also throughout our
lifetime.

"Who is this Jesus for whom we are eagerly waiting?"
is the question we meditate on this first weekend and try
to get the answer to. First of all, in the light of scriptures

and Christian tradition, we are inspired to believe that the one for whom we are waiting is not an ordinary leader as the secular world defines. Nor is he a prophet (Nabi), as our Islamic brethren consider, or one of the many incarnations of God, as our Hinduistic friends uphold. Rather, he is a person who is named Jesus Christ, the Son of God and the Lord of the universe.

In the midst of the trials and perils troubling Israel, Prophet Jeremiah was sent by God to encourage and console his people with an oracle about the wonderful days when all his promises would be fulfilled. This is what the prophet said: "In those days, at that time, I will make a just shoot spring up for David; he shall do what is right and just in the land" (Jer. 33:15). This prophecy was later understood by the church, by the inspiration of Jesus's spirit, as a foretelling of Jesus of Nazareth—who, in fact, belonged to the clan of David. Plus, the prophet was speaking not only about Israel's future—but also about the new Israel, the Church of Jesus.

In the Gospel passage we have taken for our meditation, Jesus—referring to himself as the "Son of Man," as Prophet Daniel foretold—was the one who would be coming from heaven in glory and power to judge the entire human family on their performances during their earthly life. As biblical scholars interpreted, the term "Son of Man" Jesus used was to define his dual identity of being both the "glorious Son of God" and the "suffering man of God" as well. This might have been shocking to the Israelites of his time. He repeated such flabbergasting statements many times, especially when he was standing for the trial at the Sanhedrin. Answering the question of Caiaphas whether he was the Messiah, the Son of God, *Jesus said to him in reply, 'You have said so. But I tell you: From now on, you will see the Son of Man seated at the right hand of the Power and coming on the clouds of heaven'"* (Matt. 26:64). Everyone in the Sanhedrin confirmed that he was uttering a blasphemy. But he never flinched from his standpoint; and surely, we know how such a staggering statement took him to undergo ignominious sufferings and death.

Jesus, for whom we are waiting, is also identified by his followers as the Savior of the world. The name *Jesus,* in Hebrew, means "God saves." The Israelites expected a deliverance from the bondage of slavery under the Roman Empire; they were longing for his powerful coming as their prophets had foretold. History testifies there were many in those days emerging with the name of Jesus, and they tried to work for their political liberation in violence and hatred. But this Jesus of Nazareth promised a twofold salvation— social and spiritual—that could be attained by forgiveness, love, and truth. It was a deliverance from sin and death, and his followers were convinced he gave that salvation by his sacrifice on the cross.

As we are heading to the commemoration of Jesus's first coming into this world, we must strengthen our realistic faith in the human Jesus's divine origin. Faith is indeed a leap into darkness, but not a leap into ignorance; we should know what our faith is, where it leads us to, and whom it projects. It is because of the lack of such knowledge that many among us drift away from Jesus's sheepfold. We not only should be well-informed of these truths about Jesus, but we should put it earnestly in our daily walk of life.

As Paul attests, Jesus's disciples earnestly asked and exhorted others, while they were waiting for their Lord's coming, that they should follow strenuously in the footsteps of Jesus. They should conduct themselves to

3

please God and to be blameless in holiness before our God and Father at the coming of our Lord Jesus with all his holy ones (1 Thess. 3:12–4:2). Let us be enlightened more and more in our faith toward Jesus so that we fervently and meaningfully wait for him. And when he arrives, he may find us awakened; and we may encounter him not as a stringent judge but more as a Good Shepherd who will take us with him to his chamber to partake in his eternal banquet.

SECOND WEEKEND

Second Advent Sunday
Attention! Caution! Roadwork ahead!

The Word of God came to John, the son of Zechariah, in the desert. He went throughout the whole region of the Jordan, proclaiming a baptism of repentance for the forgiveness of sins, as it is written in the book of the words of the prophet Isaiah: "A voice of one crying out in the desert: 'Prepare the way of the Lord, make straight his paths. Every valley shall be filled and every mountain and hill shall be made low. The winding roads shall be made straight, and the rough ways made smooth, and all flesh shall see the salvation of God.'" (Luke 3:1–6)

Attention! Caution! Roadwork ahead! We are familiar with such signboards as we drive on our highways and country roads. Surely, this is the theme of John the Baptist's message and that is God's Word underscores for our life—which is, personally I feel, nothing but an Advent season. When I browsed the Internet for getting to know how the modern world uses this term "roadwork," I found three usages. It means, surely, repair of roads: road construction or repair work being carried out on a section of public road, or on the utilities located near it, creating a temporary obstruction for road users. It also means "training exercise." In the sports world, it is a form of exercise consisting of long runs on roads, done especially as part of a training program. It can also refer to the work of touring. This, in the music world, is used to denote the activity of taking a band, especially a rock band, on a lengthy tour of performances. God invites us to meditate this weekend on this triple dimension of our roadwork in our Advent life.

Human life is a journey that starts at conception, but it doesn't end with "dead end." It is rather a lively pilgrimage clearly having its destination, which is glorious Jerusalem. We, the disciples of Jesus, do not join with the depressed people who feel very negatively that their lives are heading toward its horrible "dead end." Our conviction is that our life is a sort of pilgrimage marching on to a decisive goal—namely, to enter into heaven, the Holy of Holies, as Jews make their pilgrimage to Jerusalem, the Holy City. Prophet Baruch (Bar. 5:1–9) describes our pilgrimage very poetically and hopefully toward heaven symbolized by Jerusalem. Like other prophets, Baruch makes us realize that in our human endeavors of enhancing our earthly life, our God accompanies us in the liberation march from the bond of social injustice and conflicts to a spiritual realm of true justice, peace, joy, and unity of the human race.

John the Baptizer, the last prophet of the Old Testament, confirms all prophecies concerned about our life-pilgrimage and adds to them a down-to-earth explanation of it (Luke 3:1–6). He calls it our pilgrim way, where we (God and ourselves) meet together, as the "Way of the Lord." He agrees with our feelings about the rough "pilgrim way" of human life: a path full of ups and downs and depths, pits, and gorges. And its roads are winding. As Luke portrays, in the times of John and Jesus, the people's path of life was perilous and scary in all its dimensions.

Politically, people were enslaved citizens of the Roman Empire; religiously, they were surrounded by corrupted leaders who were desecrating the Holy of Holies by making it a "den of thieves." Socially, John and Jesus were born and bred in a tiny little province in the eastern part of the empire. This means they were living as members of a very minority group of Jews who were very sincere in observing God's commandments because the only hope for them to walk in the pilgrimage peacefully and joyfully is the belief in their Lord—who, as the prophet foretold, was *"leading Israel in joy by the light of his glory, with his mercy and justice for company."*

Today, we encounter the same bitter life situations as the Jews of Jesus's time had—even worse still. God invites us to go on our journey with no fear despite the hurdles and odds we face in our journey. We are fully aware of the Christian path, which we have taken as our pilgrim way to reach God's hilltop. It is very dangerous and damaged, bloody, evil-filled, full of temptations, and narrow and slippery. God tells us today that we should never be fainted or frustrated on the way, seeing how difficult it is to pass through this life journey, because God is the one who called us and mooted this pilgrimage of life. As Paul writes confidently, *"The one who began a good work in us will continue to complete it until the day of Christ Jesus"* (Phil. 1:6). We too must uphold in our hearts that our powerful, just, and merciful God in Jesus's Spirit walks with us. He is Emmanuel, "God with us."

As we walk the walk of pilgrimage, let us be vigilant and patient, unceasingly praying, and never losing hope. Plus, while we move on, traveling, let us do something about the bloody path in the society as Jesus did. But before anything we do in this matter, we should first try to level

7

and repair our own "personal life path," which would have become a path of injustice, the road of disunity, the way of violence and terrorism. As we move on to reach our heavenly goal, we should do our best to clean the disorderly and damaged and deteriorated path. Through John the Baptist in the Gospel, we are called for such radical actions to be taken by us while we are journeying toward the coming of Jesus.

THIRD WEEKEND

Third Advent Sunday
What Should We Do to Seize Christian Joy?

> *And the crowds asked him, "What then should we do?" . . . Now the people were filled with expectation, and all were asking in their hearts whether John might be the Messiah. John answered them all, saying, "I am baptizing you with water, but one mightier than I is coming. I am not worthy to loosen the thongs of his sandals. He will baptize you with the Holy Spirit and fire. His winnowing fan is in his hand to clear his threshing floor and to gather the wheat into his barn, but the chaff he will burn with unquenchable fire." Exhorting them in many other ways, he preached good news to the people.*
>
> (Luke 3:10–18)

A genuine committed Christian life is a life of joy. It cannot be anything else. According to scripture and our Church tradition, the entire Christian life is a joyful time and definitely not a gloomy time. Prophets, like Zephaniah (Zeph. 3:14–18), and apostles, like Paul (Phil. 4:4–7), were genuinely committed to God and intimately connected to his love. They were true to their religion. Therefore, they could be full of joy and express that joy in their poems, writings, and letters—inspiring their fellow men to be with the same feelings of joy. Even they make their God sing with them the song of joy. They enlist so many reasons for such joyful feelings. But one thing is very clear: namely, this joyful attitude is simply the result of their uninterrupted religious commitment to the God they worshipped.

We too, as committed disciples of Jesus and members of his religion, are supposed to be filled with this complete joy because of the kind of God we have, the kind of God Jesus revealed to us right from the very first Christmas. He is called Immanuel—that is, "God with us," "God for us," and "God on our side." A God in whom we can believe and trust as being absolutely and entirely and only good; and we believe in this kind of God even in the midst of seemingly insuperable trials and suffering. A God who is kind and merciful and understanding and considerate and constantly loving and caring. This is the beautiful, wonderful kind of God who came to us at the first Christmas, and continues to come to us, and will come to us even at the very end. And it is because we know that it is this kind of God we have that we are at ease, at peace, and therefore able to be full of joy in all of life, without any gloom or fear or guilt or anxiety. Notwithstanding even our faults and failures and weakness and blindness. Notwithstanding even our sins.

Very sadly, we observe many among us have been so little a joyful people and so much a people riddled with fear and guilt and anxiety. If we desire to be liberated from these sources of sadness to get back our original joy-filled life bestowed at our baptism, we should ask ourselves, "What is wrong with us?" And we also should ask the Lord as the Jewish crowd asked John the Baptizer, "What then should we do?" The right answer comes from God in the words of John. First, he says: *"Whoever has two tunics should share with the person who has none. And whoever has food should do likewise."* It means, accepting the gospel demands a change in one's personal conduct.

We need a radical change from a self-centered personality to a self-sharing one. We must become persons who love to share, rather than persons who are avaricious to accumulate the good things of life. Next, finger-pointing the unjust habits of tax collectors of his time, he emphasizes: *"Stop collecting more than what is prescribed."* He proposes another kind of radical change from unjust behavior to justice-oriented life. Tax collectors, in Jesus's time, had a bad reputation of paying a lump-sum to the Empire and were then left to their own devices to get back that money and make a profit besides. Such a dishonest and unjust system led to a good deal of extortion, which hurt the welfare of the people, particularly of the poor citizens.

In addition, John said: *"Do not practice extortion, do not falsely accuse anyone, and be satisfied with your wages."* It was his answer to the question raised by soldiers who were burdened with anxieties in balancing their lives. Through his saying, John recommends to people a radical change from arrogant power play to compassionate service.

While he preached through his words all the above-listed messages, he preached also another very important one by his own life. It was about the need of a radical change from a "proud-mind setup" to a "humble, melting-heart setup." He was very straightforward and humble in performing his duties as the forerunner of Christ.

One example to this is included in the Gospel passage we meditate on this weekend. When he was asked whether he was the Messiah, he never bluffed or gave any confusing answer. Rather, he was plain in saying that he was not the Messiah, even of whose sandals he was unworthy to untie. To sum up all these advices of John, to be eternally joyful is simply to lead a life of commitment to the Lord and live a godly life. And as Fr. Tony de Mello says in his book *Awareness*: "We have everything we need here and now to be happy. The problem is that we identify our happiness with people or things we don't have and often can't have."

FOURTH WEEKEND

Fourth Advent Sunday
In Order to Make Our Joy Complete

During those days, Mary set out and traveled to the hill country in haste to a town of Judah, where she entered the house of Zechariah and greeted Elizabeth. When Elizabeth heard Mary's greeting, the infant leaped in her womb, and Elizabeth, filled with the Holy Spirit, cried out in a loud voice and said, "Most blessed are you among women, and blessed is the fruit of your womb. And how does this happen to me, that the mother of my Lord should come to me? For at the moment the sound of your greeting reached my ears, the infant in my womb leaped for joy." (Luke 1:39–44)

Many of us confuse with the terms "happiness" and "joy." For example, the fact that at certain days, certain moments, or even seasons, we tend to feel like we are floating in the air with euphoria. We think and say we are joyful. No, it isn't joy. We are merely happy, because our zest stays only for a while and then fades away once the gala time comes to an end. The reason the feelings fade is that we are created not just for happiness but also for joy. There is a vast difference between the two. Happiness comes from happenings, but joy is a distinctively holy and religious experience that springs up from deep within a faith-filled heart. Joy remains untouched by outward circumstances, and it is not extinguished even by suffering, struggle, or sorrow.

It is this joy Jesus came to give to us. He affirmed to his disciples: *"I have said these things to you so that my joy may be in you, and that your joy may be complete."* Jesus came on earth to give not mere earthly happiness but joy that is eternal happiness. Throughout his life, he behaved as a "jolly good fellow." This character was shown by him already while he was in his mother's womb. In the Gospel passage we have taken for this weekend's meditation, we hear two pregnant women greeting each other and the baby Jesus from inside Mary psychically and spiritually, in a way sharing his joy with baby John who was in Elizabeth, who then burst out saying, "For at the moment the sound of your greeting reached my ears, the infant in my womb leaped for joy." This joyful mind-set stayed with Jesus till his last breath. Nothing would deter him coming out of his inner genuine joy. In addition to his promise of bestowing us "complete joy," he demonstrated the way to covet this wonderful gift.

First, he testifies this is possible only when we totally surrender to our God, the Creator. The Letter to the Hebrews spells out this truth of how Jesus began his span of life in this world. *"When Christ came into the world, he said: 'Sacrifice and offering you did not desire but a body you prepared for me; in holocausts and sin offerings you took no delight.' Then I said, 'As is written of me in the scroll, behold, I come to do your will, O God . . .'"* (Heb. 10:5–10). Jesus wants us to hold an attitude in our lives as he said yes to his Father when he came to this world. For that yes, he had to pay a tremendous price by sacrificing his very self, his life, and all his glory and identity.

His sacrifice is indescribable. His identity and nature, as we strongly uphold, is divine. As Prophet Micah proclaimed (Mic. 5:1–4), Jesus is the ruler in Israel; his origin is from of old. He will rule with power; his rule will reach to the ends of the world. He is also called "peace," not just a peacemaker or prince of peace but source of peace. Despite all these highest qualities, Jesus said yes to God's will and emptied himself, detached himself from his true identity and accepted to be born as a slave. And Paul wouldn't stop writing about his admiration for this humble and sacrificial attitude of Jesus in all his Letters.

Following his footsteps and messages of joy, we witness in human history how millions of people gained the "complete joy." Mary, the mother of Jesus, first bowing down to her Creator, said, *"Behold the handmaid of the Lord, be it done unto me according to your word."* And for such a humble gesture, she experienced this joy as she sang, *"My spirit rejoices in God my savior."* Along with so many disciples of Jesus, John the Baptizer, with all his humble surrender to his God, was daring enough to bow down to a new preacher and teacher in the person of Jesus and pointing out to Jesus as the Lamb of God, smilingly admitting: *"The one who has the bride is the bridegroom; the best man, who stands and listens for him, rejoices greatly at the bridegroom's voice. So this joy of mine has been made complete. He must increase; I must decrease"* (John 3:29–30). The Apostle Paul was always joyful in his ministry. He learned how to live and rejoice in every circumstance. While he was in prison, he would write with exuberance: *"Rejoice in the Lord always! I say it again. Rejoice!"*

Every one of us craves for true joy. But true joy can't be defined in words, nor can it be measured or tested in any scientific lab. It can only be experienced. Most of it exists in the spiritual realm. We know by our past lives that we, by ourselves, cannot experience such true and complete joy; nor can any other human being or pet or thing supplement it. This is why Jesus expects us to always approach God, who is the source and store of that joy. Joy becomes possible only after we lend ourselves to his Spirit. And finding out how selfish we are and how we live our daily lives filled with injustice and hatred, we should start working on those imperfections.

Christmas
Peace to the Good-Willed

In those days, a decree went out from Caesar Augustus that the whole world should be enrolled. This was the first enrollment, when Quirinius was governor of Syria . . . While they were there, the time came for her to have her child, and she gave birth to her firstborn son. She wrapped him in swaddling clothes and laid him in a manger, because there was no room for them in the inn. Now there were shepherds in that region living in the fields and keeping the night watch over their flock. The angel of the Lord appeared to them, and the glory of the Lord shone around them, and they were struck with great fear. The angel said to them, "Do not be afraid; for behold, I proclaim to you good news of great joy that will be for all the people. For today, in the city of David, a savior has been born for you, who is Messiah and Lord. And this will be a sign for you: you will find an infant wrapped in swaddling clothes and lying in a manger." And suddenly, there was a multitude of the heavenly host with the angel, praising God and saying: "Glory to God in the highest and on earth peace to those on whom his favor rests." (Luke 2:1–14)

The feast we celebrate today is very unique of its own. Though Jesus's birth was as any other human birth in Palestine, it has its specialty. First, Jesus's birth was a history. In the Gospel reading taken for our meditation this weekend, Luke offers us a tiny historical background of Jesus's birth. According to him, Jesus's birth occurred at the time of Caesar Augustus, as the Roman emperor, and when Quirinius was governor of Syria. Secondly, Jesus's birth, which we celebrate today, is a story. In every human's birth, except their parents, all others do not know fully the real fact of one's birth. Parents would know all the things happened in conception and birth historically. All others are able to get only its stories as told by parents or relatives. It was the same way with Jesus's birth. Though it was historical, only Mary, his mother, knew well its entire history. When she and Joseph joined together and shared the history of their son's birth, it surely reached to their mind as stories. Only two evangelists write in their books a few stories about the birth of Jesus.

The third wondrous element found in Jesus's birth is it is a mystery. It contains too many truths and issues that cannot be easily digested or accepted by ordinary human beings: Jesus was conceived by the Holy Spirit in the Virgin Mary's womb (Luke 1:26–38). From his conception, Christ's humanity is filled with the Holy Spirit, for God "gives him the Spirit without measure" (John 3:34). Professing this baby Jesus as the grace from God, Paul writes: *"For the grace of God has appeared, saving all and training us to reject godless ways and worldly desires and to live temperately, justly, and devoutly in this age . . ."* (Titus

2:11–14). Another breathtaking dimension of mystery is how such a prosperous and glorious Son of God was born in a humble stable, into a poor family; and simple shepherds were the first witnesses to this event. In this poverty, heaven's glory was made manifest.

Jesus's birth—though it has been a history, story, and mystery—informs us of an important lesson regarding our need of the day. Namely, if we desire to get God's "fuller life" in this world and the world to come, we should read between the lines in these stories of Jesus's birth and find out the condition God puts before us to receive his life. Luke, in his narration, mentions one event that is very normal and ordinary at any poor baby's birth. That is, *"An infant wrapped in swaddling clothes and laid in a manger."* It is three times repeated by the Evangelist to emphasize its importance as a perfect message announced to all who celebrate Jesus's birth.

Glory belongs only to the Supreme Being, God. With angels, we love to sing *"Glory to God in the highest."* We want our God to be all in glory, in power, and in victory. We like to see him always stand erect—no failure, no lack of anything. When we want him to come to us in our midst, we look for him in the same glorious status. But the Bible tells us we would die if we saw him that way in our mortal body, so he took ordinary human form. He came as an infant: helpless, vulnerable, weak, simple, and poor. God asserted that until we digest this "intolerable" revelation of God's glory, we cannot get peace or remain in peace. He knew it would be hard for us; therefore, he presented a positive message again through the angels, who added a verse to their hymns: *"Peace to the people of goodwill."* Only good-willed people, who dream of greater things in life from Above, will accept this hard truth of seeing God as an infant, finding his glory in poverty and love. God's unique glory at the birth of Jesus shines. He highlighted it as being poor in spirit, being committed to life out of love, and reciprocating love for hatred, forgiveness in the place of retaliation, and being truthful in the time of trials.

This is why St. Francis of Assisi prayed in front of the crib, which he himself built for the first time: *"Make me a channel of your peace. Where there is hatred, let me sow love. Where there is despair, let me bring hope. Where there is darkness, let me bring light. And where there is sadness, let me sow joy."* This hymn was generated from the heart of Francis, who clearly knew: *"It is in giving that we receive, it is in pardoning that we are pardoned, and it is in dying that we are born to eternal life."*

FIFTH WEEKEND

Feast of Holy Family
Holy Family is a Team bonded by God's Will

> *When his parents saw him, they were*
> *astonished, and his mother said to him,*
> *"Son, why have you done this to us? Your*
> *father and I have been looking for you*
> *with great anxiety." And he said to them,*
> *"Why were you looking for me? Did you*
> *not know that I must be in my Father's*
> *house?" But they did not understand what*
> *he said to them. He went down with them*
> *and came to Nazareth, and was obedient*
> *to them; and his mother kept all these*
> *things in her heart. And Jesus advanced*
> *[in] wisdom and age and favor before God*
> *and man.*

"Family" is defined as a fundamental social group in society, typically consisting of two parents and their children. These members of a household live under one roof. It is a group of persons who share common ancestry. This means it is a group of individuals derived from a common stock: the family of human beings. This is a right description of what we used to call the traditional family. And its dignity has been maintained in the church for centuries and offered the Family of Nazareth to all families as their role model to be intact and holy. In this modern world, such a form of family system is becoming a smaller and smaller majority. We encounter different forms and shapes of family, such as single-parent families, foster families, blended families, etc. Many Christians perceive that these kinds of "postmodern families" cannot be called "holy" families because of their drifting from the original traditional family system.

In the Gospel of Luke, we read about the family Jesus was born and bred in. Joseph, according to tradition, was a widower who married Mary; therefore, all children from his previous marriage were esteemed as stepsons and stepdaughters to Mary, and stepbrothers and stepsisters to Jesus. And Jesus was a foster son to Joseph and not real son. Hence, the Family of Nazareth cannot be included as one among "traditional" families. This sort of departure from traditional style of family-living can be traced in the lives of many biblical characters.

For example, Prophet Samuel's family (1 Sam. 1:20–28): Hannah, his mother, leaves her son entirely in the hands of high priest Eli at the temple. No more then he belonged to his family. Jesus's behavior both in his teenage years and adulthood as well seems to be again telling us that living under one roof is not going to make the family holy. Very sadly, Jesus abruptly leaves his mom one day, telling her he wants to do the will of his Father. Thus, we see how all those families even four thousand years back did not comply with the right definition of a family. Nonetheless, the church upholds the integrity and dignity of the traditional family system under the guidance of Jesus's Spirit. Therefore, we have to search for the true definition and meaning of "holy family."

The Family of Nazareth became holy not because it was up to the characteristics of a traditional family—but rather, because it was built and maintained as the meeting place of heaven and earth, where God reached out to us humans in an act of bonding. From the few narrations we read about this family in Luke and Matthew, we observe the strong and indissoluble bond maintained among the members of that family, always tied with God's love and truth. A family we create or belong to means not just living under one same roof, nor is its togetherness bound by laws and principles, nor a place where goods and possessions are distributed evenly and justly. But it is "living together in spirit and in truth." It is the "communing of feelings, temperaments, knowledge, and the very self with each other mutually."

Moreover, Jesus's family became holy because Jesus, Mary, and Joseph were bonded, grouped, united on the basis of one ultimate principle—namely, the will of God. We discover more of this in Jesus, who possessed an incessant obsession of doing God's will from the moment he entered into this world. In the Gospel, he reveals it to his parents: *"Why were you looking for me? Did you not know that I must be in my Father's house?"* When his mom came to visit him while he was performing his public ministry, he is quoted saying: *"Who are my mother and (my) brothers?" And looking around at those seated in the circle, he said, "Here are my mother and my brothers. (For) whoever does the will of God is my brother and sister and mother."* This is how Jesus understood and preached the true family concept. Any togetherness other than this is simply fake, deceptive, and sometimes very dangerous.

Jesus wants us to treasure and cherish any kind of family situation we have been led in. As John proclaims in his Letter, we should *"see what love the Father has bestowed on us that we may be called the children of God. Yet so we are"* (1 John 3–1). And we should love one another just as he commanded us. Some would esteem the appearance of a home more than the happy life within the home. If we are in the habit of passing judgment on family, community, and people at large, we have probably lost touch with the more central values of love. The Holy Family of Nazareth should be a model of an ideal family life, where the fully grown mind-setup of loving sincerely, serving selflessly, and sacrificing totally takes origin and grows.

FIFTH WEEKEND SPECIAL

New Year's Day
"Let Us Be Thrice Blessed This Year"

*The Lord said to Moses . . . "The Lord bless
you and keep you! The Lord let his face
shine upon you, and be gracious to you!
The Lord look upon you kindly and give
you peace!"* (Num. 6:22–27)

"Well begun, half done" is a golden rule for successful
people who get very good results in their lives. They always
begin their undertakings with great interest, full of trust
and hope, and being blessed by God and their neighbors.
They make sure their efforts start at a good time, a good
place, a good opportunity, and with a good plan and
sufficient financing—plus with good attitudes and efficient
helping hands. Once they begin their business with these
blessings, the entire project reaches to its completion as
they willed. The same is true with this New Year's start. It
should start well so that the rest of the year would be happy
and fruitful.

It is for this reason that on the first weekend of
this year, we would have gathered in the churches. As
Christians, instead of making recourse to human power
or any worldly wisdom, we want to start the year with
the Lord's graces and blessings. Those who are seriously
digging into the scriptures will find numerous blessings
promised by God.

Today, at the onset of another year, for our "home-in"
meditation, let us read and reflect on a relevant passage

from the Book of Numbers. It is our Christian faith, as God blessed the Old Testament people of God through his messengers and elders—we too have been blessed by God abundantly through our faith-filled adherence and commitment to his love-call, plus through our active participation ritually and actually in his church's discipleship. The blessings are triple: priestly, kingly, and prophetic. So let us bless ourselves with this positive-faith thinking as we start this New Year.

Many evil things would have occurred in the previous year. So many unexpected things would have jolted us, shaken us, or shocked us. But still, we hold on to the words of God about his blessings. Let us put aside the past. The future only should be in our eyes. As we do not look back constantly while we drive our cars in order to be safe and we only see what is coming back to us through the side or rear mirrors, so shall we use the past as a side effect to our future orchestra. The past failures, and even sins, will assist us in straightening out our attitudes and our decision-making process. Otherwise, the past is dangerous if it is given much importance in our lives. The promised blessings are there in abundance.

At the same time, we too should know the same God has included in these blessings another miraculous one. He tells Moses that he is imparting the power to Aaron and his sons to bless his people. Aaron and his sons were chosen by God and anointed by him to act as priests in his name. In other words, they were chosen to be the channel of blessing from God to the people. Each one of us, through our baptism, is called to act like priests in between God and our community. As Jesus became the priest of God, so we are made into priests through our baptismal anointing.

We hold a power to bless each other as mother, father, brother, sister, husband, wife, leader, or friend. It is the blessing of ability to bless others, of the power to lead and manage, and of the luck to hold an eternally propitious word of fortune—namely, we are predestined for good and good alone to enjoy everything that is good born out of his love."

SIXTH WEEKEND

Feast of Epiphany
***To Become His Epiphanies, We
Need to Digest His Epiphany***

*When Jesus was born in Bethlehem of
Judea, in the days of King Herod, behold,
magi from the east arrived in Jerusalem,
saying, "Where is the newborn king of
the Jews? We saw his star at its rising
and have come to do him homage." When
King Herod heard this, he was greatly
troubled, and all Jerusalem with him.
Assembling all the chief priests and the
scribes of the people, he inquired of them
where the Messiah was to be born . . .
After their audience with the king, they
set out. And behold, the star that they
had seen at its rising preceded them,
until it came and stopped over the place
where the child was. They were overjoyed
at seeing the star, and on entering the
house, they saw the child with Mary, his
mother. They prostrated themselves and
did him homage. Then they opened their
treasures and offered him gifts of gold,
frankincense, and myrrh. And having
been warned in a dream not to return to
Herod, they departed for their country by
another way.* (Matt. 2:1–12)

The Lord invites us this weekend, as we just began the New Year, to meditate on his Epiphany to us, especially to those of us who were once called the Gentiles. The term "epiphany" is probably an alteration of the Greek *epiphaneia*, which means "appearing, manifesting, or showing forth." Historically, it has been used to point out exclusively to the manifestations of a supernatural or divine reality. In modern usage, it denotes any moment of great or sudden revelation, in which humans strikingly perceive something in a new and clear perspective.

It is a historical fact that from the day of creation, humans have been craving for God's chilling and thrilling manifestation in his power and glory. Not only the Gospel writers but all the apostles and disciples who belonged to Jesus's team in the first century were inspired by Jesus's godly Spirit to go through his life's events, his sayings, and his accomplishments to discover what and how he manifested his identity and nature. In other words, every step, every moment, every lip movement was an epiphany of his self. *"When you read this, you can understand my insight into the mystery of Christ, which was not made known to human beings in other generations as it has now been revealed to his holy apostles and prophets by the Spirit, that the Gentiles are coheirs, members of the same body, and copartners in the promise in Christ Jesus through the gospel"* (Eph. 3:2–6).

The biblical story we have taken for our meditation is from the Gospel of Matthew, whose main aim for narrating it was to proclaim that Jesus was born not only for the Jews but also the Gentiles. We are told by Matthew that a unique manifestation of divine glory through Baby Jesus was offered to the Gentiles. We read the Magi, who came from East, offered to Baby Jesus three gifts of gold, frankincense, and myrrh. According to traditional interpretation, those gifts were the symbols that contained the content of his epiphany. The gift of gold symbolized the kingship of Jesus, the incense expressed his divinity, and the myrrh foretold of Jesus as a typical human who would undergo passion and death.

We observe in the New Testament books and in church tradition that Jesus had manifested the presence of invisible God in him by the events of his life: as a helpless child lying in a manger and as a young man dying on the cross, the ultimate revelation that God's glory is love. This means that Jesus is the revelation of God as one who offers himself to us in love. At his birth, we encounter the revelation of the purpose of his Incarnation: that God and we, God's creatures, might enjoy each other in the embrace of love. We too uphold in our religion that in Jesus's birth, the Old Testament prophecies about the redeeming Messiah were fulfilled. Referring to the arrival of the Magi, who represented humanity from all corners of the globe, Isaiah wrote: *"Nations shall walk by your light, kings by the radiance of your dawning. Raise your eyes and look about; they all gather and come to you . . ."* (Isa. 60:1–6)

This story takes us back to our day-to-day life, in which God continues to manifest himself in glory, power, wisdom, and love through Jesus's presence. Our belief in this matter is based on the promises of Jesus that he would be with us till the end of ages. He has promised to come in the forms of neighbors, the needy, the enemies, the sinners, and in our community bonded in faith and prayer. We also know he manifests himself in natural resources, creative achievements of humans, natural disasters, and other social events. He too is present in each and every one of us in our inner sanctuary and manifests himself through inspirations, inner conscience, creative thoughts, visions, dreams, and certain mystic experiences.

Unfortunately, there are many among us who do not still want to accept our spiritual worth and our marvelous capacity to see the manifestations of God in our midst. This is because of two reasons. One, we are not humble and poor in spirit; rather, we behave hardheadedly like King Herod. Two, we don't come to terms with the inspiration of God for perfection and don't dare to change our usual path of life as the Magi obeyed the angel's advice. Only when we are drawn by the manifestations of Christ and modify and purify our life path can we also become the manifestations of his presence for others.

Feast of Lord's Baptism
"Ritual Is Effective until It Blends with Homework"

After all the people had been baptized and Jesus also had been baptized and was praying, heaven was opened and the Holy Spirit descended upon him in bodily form like a dove. And a voice came from heaven, "You are my beloved Son; with you I am well pleased." (Luke 3:21–22)

In the event of baptism, we observe Jesus publicly giving a total commitment to his God. It is true he had already given this commitment in privacy as we read in Hebrews 10:5–7, "When he came into the world, he said: 'Sacrifice and offering you did not desire, but a body you prepared for me; holocausts and sin offerings you took no delight in. As is written of me in the scroll, Behold, I come to do your will, O God.'" He had waited for this moment for thirty years. Already, he proved himself as an obedient, humble, patient, and loving human person while he spent his years with his mother and family and community at Nazareth. Now he demonstrates it symbolically, or sacramentally, outside by an available religious ceremony. His personal devotion and interior commitment to his God, Emmanuel, inside of him was made visible to the God outside of him. He uses the religious ceremony available at that time to profess his commitment to God and to initiate himself into the community life in the Kingdom of God.

He dreamed to be a winner in his life; so he used baptism as his first step of immersing himself totally in the hands of God and into the depths of his physical, social, and spiritual life. He was ready to start his winning journey to face the reality of life.

Undoubtedly, Jesus already knew what was in store for him in this journey. With his humble surrender and his simple acknowledgment of his position in his community, he courageously accepted to be a suffering servant. He submitted to the mandate of God to go forward to establish justice in the world, to enlighten men and women with his interior light so that everyone would get freedom from imprisonment and ignorance supplied by the Evil Force. He willingly agreed to that horrible role filled with hurdles and difficulties. He was ready to take this hard road all the way to Calvary, even to be murdered there.

What we see in this scenario of Jesus taking his first bold step to his public life is how God anoints him on the spot with his Holy Spirit. Plus God the Father assures Jesus's conviction from his early childhood about his identity queries: "Who am I?" and "What is my relationship with God?" "Am I God's Son?" As Luke writes, God acknowledges Jesus's worth and identity and shouted out with his thunderous voice from the sky: *"You are my beloved Son; with you I am well pleased."*

This event baptism in our Lord's life reminds us of our own baptism, either as infants or adults. As John the Baptist foretold, we, the followers of Jesus, are also initiated into his discipleship by the baptism not only of water but also of the fire and the Spirit. Jesus and his church expect that we too might experience at our baptism whatever Jesus had experienced at his baptism. Jesus becomes our pattern and role model in our Christian lives.

What Jesus and his church advise is that mere ritual baptism won't do justice to its miraculous effects, as it did to the Lord, until we do the homework as Jesus did before and after his baptism. He had been constantly in touch with God inside of him by continuous prayers and religious practices; he was faithful to his commitment to God and religion first in his hidden and private life. Then, and then only, he demonstrated it through sacramental signs like baptism and continued to keep it intact by his strenuous obedience to his Father's will.

Most of us have been baptized very early in our babyhood. There were proxies who responded yes to God on our behalf. Cradle Catholics must work harder to realize the real effects of baptism. Good-willed people therefore try to renew their baptismal commitment in the name of "second baptism." Let's join them, and once we receive the Spirit's gifts, let's try our best to perform all our activities as mom, dad, officer, nurse, teacher, etc.—coming out of not mere natural talent, need, or natural love but from that of the commitment we promised at our baptism. Then we will reap the real fruits that God designed for us as our destiny. We will be going about doing good with the power of God as Jesus was. Let us follow the advice of the legendary labor agitator Mother Jones: "Pray for the dead, but fight like hell for the living."

EIGHTH WEEKEND

Second Sunday of the Year
"Let's Celebrate Life Together"

On the third day, there was a wedding in Cana in Galilee, and the mother of Jesus was there. Jesus and his disciples were also invited to the wedding. When the wine ran short, the mother of Jesus said to him, "They have no wine." [And] Jesus said to her, "Woman, how does your concern affect me? My hour has not yet come." His mother said to the servers, "Do whatever he tells you." (John 2:1–11)

Let us look around the place where the wedding event at Cana happened. We see a variety of people, various things, different roles and identities. Jesus and Mary, the disciples of Jesus, and various relatives and friends as guests were sitting there on one side; on the other, you see the bridegroom and the bride, the best man and maid of honor, and all the servants and cooks, plus the common folk who have come to witness the wedding event out of curiosity. All are different from each other in their statuses, relationships, roles, characters, needs, and so on. But there is one thing that connects them together, and that is the celebration aspect of that moment of a main event happening in human life.

Three sudden twists happen during the happiest moment, which seem to be turning points in that celebration. First, it is found out that there is no wine to serve the guests. The second turning point is when Mary requests Jesus, her son, to do something about this unwanted happening. Jesus seems to turn down her request. The third twist is water being changed into wine, and with even better quality. We know how all the characters who participated in that moment of celebration would feel and experience different feelings such as sad, shocking, pitying, and murmuring and so on. Yet a few among them are there who—like Mary, the mother of Jesus—follow God's tips to maintain the balanced spirit. Thanks to them, that event again turns out to be a celebration.

This is what every one of us face in life encounters in our homes, parishes, communities, nations, and the world. Look at the horrible earthquakes, tsunamis, tornados, and other terroristic and political wars through which the entire global society has been thrown into a tailspin.

Millions die and billions go without meals, shelters, medications, and still other millions are living in no-man's lands as refugees. Watch keenly how the celebration in their lives has been destroyed. Yet people there, as well as those around the world, pour out their love and compassion and hold on to God's greatness and goodness to bring back the celebration spirit once again in that deplorable environment.

As Mary advised the servers during a critical life situation, our Christian conscience urges us, at such moments in today's world, to "do whatever Jesus tells us to do." Everyone born and bred in this world by the Creator is designed to celebrate the godly life bestowed unto us. A genuine celebration of life cannot be realized without being together with our human family. We should not be alone like a lonely man or an island. We should live as a member of a group, family, community—not as mere nominal registered members, but being totally involved in that community and becoming an integral part of it. Though we are different in many ways—especially in our IQ, DNA, heredity, culture, and background of formation and education, and especially possessing various talents different from each other—we have to work together in times of peril. The more we are involved in assisting the suffering victims to rise up and to celebrate their lives, the happier would be our own life-celebration.

NINTH WEEKEND

Third Sunday of the Year
We Are the Ministers of God's Words Today Living

> *In the square in front of the Water Gate, Ezra read out of the book from daybreak till midday, in the presence of the men, the women, and those children old enough to understand; and all the people listened attentively to the book of the law . . . Ezra opened the scroll so that all the people might see it, for he was standing higher than any of the people. When he opened it, all the people stood. Ezra blessed the Lord, the great God, and all the people, their hands raised high, answered, "Amen, amen!" Then they knelt down and bowed before the Lord, their faces to the ground.*
> (Neh. 8:3–6)

"May you live long, live strong, and live happy!" This is the wish of all promoters of various medicines and diet programs you find in their weblogs. It is a traditional belief of almost all world religions that the scriptures they received from their founders or forebears are sacred—generated by God's Spirit and effective manuals, or guides, for humans to reach out to the Supreme Being. Judeo-Christians are not exempt from this. Every book in the Bible bases all its proposals, strategies, and exhortations on the singular faith that, as we read in the Psalms, "They are spirit and life to us."

Surely we, as humans, need spirit and life in order to live long, live strong, and live happy. When Ezra, the priest-scribe, read the words from the Jewish scriptures to the gathered assembly so that those words would become the source of their life, the cause of their union and the bond that would forever unite them with God, they bowed and accepted every bit of those words.

This event reminds us of the first appearance of Jesus in a synagogue. As Luke narrates, Jesus took the Old Testament scroll of the prophet Isaiah and combined two texts to deliver the words that would outline his life agenda. At the end, he added that all that was prophesied by Isaiah in the Old Testament scriptures were fulfilled in him (Luke 4:18–21). In other words, through New Testament books, we are made to believe, besides the amazing power of God's Word, that Jesus of Nazareth had come down as the Word of God in whom all that had been proclaimed by God in the past was fulfilled. Unmistakably, Jesus's words of the Word became more powerful by the fact that he spent his life and went to his death in order to fulfill them. Through Jesus's words and works, the Good News was heard by the poor, captives were liberated, the blind began to see, and the oppressed went free.

The amazing achievements, realized for the past twenty centuries by Jesus's disciples, were possible only because they possessed and preserved God's words, which are contained both in Old Testament Books and mainly in Jesus the Word himself. Those words were burning in their hearts unceasingly. Plus they were all transformed into being, moving, and doing as the true replica of God's Word as Jesus did. This was possible not just reading, memorizing, and repeating God's words as litany and ejaculatory prayers. The disciples in the past tried their best digesting them spiritually through meditation and prayer in solitude.

What we notice in those disciples is very unthinkable to us. They read or heard the words of God as a group of one with one heart, and they accepted these with no dissension among themselves. Actually, they didn't play politics in this spiritual matter. Anyone who has watched an American president addressing the Congress knows the leader will get a varied reception. Members of that political party will be quick to applaud, while those of a different persuasion will be silent, refusing to show their approval. No such partisanship should be present among those who gather to listen to God's words. Look at the Israelites. When Ezra read God's words, all were attentive, and all agreed to accept the word of the Law with a wholehearted double amen. Without such unity, the Word of God would never be effective first within us; and then when we utter our words of advice, suggestion, warning, or appeal, they will never have a fruitful and longstanding effect on our listeners.

Moreover, these disciples never stopped at mere preaching and proclaiming God's words by their lips. Like the Master, they were able to establish a relationship with the least ones of society, such that they were given the desire and the strength to try to break the chains that robbed them of their freedom. This is how the words of Jesus of Nazareth became "glad tidings to the poor." We who live in the interim between Jesus's first impact on earth and the coming of his ultimate impact are charged with carrying out his agenda. We are to be good news, as he was, in the very manner of our being and living.

TENTH WEEKEND

Fourth Sunday of the Year
Divine Love Makes All the Difference

The word of the Lord came to me, saying:
"Before I formed you in the womb, I knew
you. Before you were born, I dedicated
you, a prophet to the nations I appointed
you. For it is I this day who have made
you a fortified city, a pillar of iron, a wall
of brass." (Jer. 1:4–5, 17–19)

Many years back, I read an interesting news piece in the media about the death of a retired schoolteacher named Harriet Richardson Ames. She was a hundred years old. It was told that she had a "bucket list" of dreams for her life. She was the kind of person that every parent would want their first-graders to have as a teacher, very loving and caring. She always wanted to be the best that she could be. The last item on that list was to earn her bachelor's degree in education. To the one who visited her a few weeks before she died, she cried aloud, "If I die tomorrow, I'll know I'll die happy, because my degree's in the works." Finally, her dream came true. She got it from the local college board, which bestowed her that degree on the basis of her educational services with love. The diploma was handed over to her at her bedside, and the day after receiving it, she peacefully died.

Every human being born in this world has got a bucket list of dreams as this lady had. Every disciple of Jesus surely is expected by God to hold such a bucket list of

Rev. Benjamin A Vima

dreams for our human survival and satisfaction. However, in order to win the race, to fight the good fight, and finally, to covet the crown of victory at the end of life, the same God wants us to add one more important dream to that bucket list. That should be both as the first and the last dream to be accomplished in each one's life. And that dream is to become a prophet—namely, to be a man/woman of God.

Prophets, like Jeremiah, confirm themselves in the light of God's revelation that they are born for greater things. They are called to be prophets—namely, to be men of God and women of God, dedicated only to God as his messengers or liaisons. Actually, when Jeremiah wrote those words we meditate on today, he was living in a moment of great suffering in which he had realized the failure of his mission. Suddenly, he felt divinely inspired to recall the memory of the original grace in order to draw strength from it against disappointment.

What we notice in the lives of prophets in the Bible is when they were dedicated to God, they also dedicated themselves to God's sons and daughters. Preserving the high esteem God thrust within them about themselves, prophets plunged themselves into the troubled waters of earthly life, however dirty these might be. In this regard, Jesus, the greatest of all the prophets, gives an example to us. As soon as he enthusiastically proclaimed to the public his "manifesto" (which we meditated on last weekend), we observe the opposition started rising against him. Unlike many leaders who enjoyed what had been called a honeymoon period after taking on the burden of authority, Jesus seemed to have gone straight from the proverbial frying pan into the fire. No sooner had he amazed his listeners with his stated agenda of good news, healing, and liberation than his detractors began to attack him, criticizing him for his all-too-familiar origins and for his willingness to offer his gifts to the heavily non-Jewish population of Capernaum before he did so for his hometown friends and neighbors.

We should take the challenges as they come with audacity and, even with some sort of freakiness, enter into the battlefield or marketplace of the world. As Jesus and the other prophets, we would encounter different whimsical reactions of our people. Sometimes they would "speak highly of us and would be amazed at the gracious words that came from our mouth"; many times, they might suspect and underestimate our identity; and several times, they would be filled with fury to hurl us down headlong (Luke 4:22–29). If, as real prophets, we are filled with the love of God and of our neighbors, we can take the challenges come what may.

We usually love to hear and hold very warmly all the positive things told by God about our identity, and we take pride in it, calling ourselves the chosen race, the royal priesthood, and people set apart; and precisely, we are called to be prophets. However, when God expects us to wear "agape" love as our main boot to walk in life, it surely hurts us, because love-matter always disciplines, curtails our freedom, our independence; and it always kills our self-centered gratification. Love is indeed a "dreadful task." The Russian writer Fyodor Dostoyevsky describes love in this way: "Love in action is a harsh and dreadful thing." Jesus and the other prophets were fully aware of this. As modern-day prophets, let us grasp this. In small things as in great ones, love makes all the difference.

Fifth Sunday of the Year
Building Up Our Strength

After he had finished speaking, he said to Simon, "Put out into deep water and lower your nets for a catch." Simon said in reply, "Master, we have worked hard all night and have caught nothing, but at your command I will lower the nets." When they had done this, they caught a great number of fish, and their nets were tearing. They signaled to their partners in the other boat to come to help them. They came and filled both boats so that they were in danger of sinking. When Simon Peter saw this, he fell at the knees of Jesus and said, "Depart from me, Lord, for I am a sinful man." For astonishment at the catch of fish they had made seized him and all those with him, and likewise James and John, the sons of Zebedee, who were partners of Simon. Jesus said to Simon, "Do not be afraid; from now on you will be catching men." When they brought their boats to the shore, they left everything and followed him. (Luke 5:4–11)

In one of my Religious Communications classes at Loyola, Chicago, during our question time, some of us asked our Jesuit professor a childlike question (most of us were still babies in our spirituality at that time): *When God and humans communicate to each other, what actions and reactions are going on between the two persons?* It was a relevant issue, we thought, because during that class hour, we were studying on human interpersonal communications. Our professor smilingly said that it was a wonderful question. And he added, "At every moment of our lives, God communicates with us in whatever environment or condition we may live in. But at times, when he needs humans for his 'creative and redemptive agenda,' he speaks to them in an intense and intimate communication technique." Then he went on describing some such events narrated in the Bible. One of them is what we have taken for today's meditation.

In this remarkable incident, first we notice that the Son of God, performing a miracle, offers to the human disciples a glimpse of his glory, holiness, and power. The same is true when God appeared to his chosen messengers like Prophet Isaiah (Isa. 6:1–8). God communicated himself to Isaiah as the Lord seated on a high and lofty throne, surrounded by his angels singing "holy, holy, holy." Together with this, Isaiah saw the frame of the door as it shook, and the house was filled with smoke.

Secondly, we observe the Communicator God in Jesus; when his receivers are found trembling and fearing, he encourages them to rise up. When Peter feels that way, Jesus comes to him and encourages him with a positive prophecy: *"Do not be afraid; from now on, you will be catching men."* In the same manner, while the prophet had stumbled and considered himself very low and humble, God—through an angel—touched the mouth of Isaiah with purifying fire and said, *"See, now that this has touched your lips, your wickedness is removed, your sin purged."*

The third action of God in his interpersonal encounter with his chosen ones is that straightaway he calls them to follow him in his footsteps, if they had been chosen by the Divine ordinance already; plus he too begins to share with them his strength and power. "Follow me" is the call of Jesus to Peter; the prophet too sensed holy God was calling him to go out to humanity on God's behalf.

Now let us go through the reactions of the human receiver standing on the side of this unthinkable interpersonal communication event. Whenever God's chosen ones experience the immense power of God in Jesus, they feel unworthy and try to resist even God's call. As the Gospel underlines, Peter falls at the knees of Jesus and says, *"Depart from me, Lord, for I am a sinful man."* Isaiah does the same, crying out, *"Woe is me, I am doomed! For I am a man of unclean lips, living among a people of unclean lips; yet my eyes have seen the King, the Lord of hosts!"*

Once God's effective and intimate communication encounters humans, the one only reaction is simply a total surrender to the Almighty. Look at Peter. With his friends, he immediately leaves everything and follows Jesus. And in the Old Testament, we read that as soon as Isaiah heard the calling of God, he took personal interest in it and volunteered to go as God directed him. *"Then I heard the voice of the Lord saying, 'Whom shall I send? Who will go for us?' 'Here I am,' I said; 'send me!'"*

Every one of us is called by God at every moment of our lives, as he is standing at our gate and knocking at our door—especially at times when we truly and honestly give him a specific time of solitude exclusively for him. He deals with us as he dealt with Peter and Isaiah and other holy men and women. God calls us sometimes to what may seem like impossible work. But when we listen with the intention of saying yes and doing what we can, he provides what we need. We have to hold the same spirit of these three men and say with the Psalmist: *"The Lord's right hand saves us. He builds up strength within us; and he will complete what he has done for us"* (Ps. 138).

TWELFTH WEEKEND

First Lenten Sunday
The Tighter the Clinging to God,
the Speedier the Flinging of Temptations

> *Filled with the Holy Spirit, Jesus returned*
> *from the Jordan and was led by the Spirit*
> *into the desert for forty days . . . He ate*
> *nothing during those days, and when they*
> *were over, he was hungry. The devil said*
> *to him . . .* (Luke 4:1–13)

Christian life is a journey, a pilgrimage, a voyage to eternity, a leap into darkness—but always in a deserted land. That was how our Lord's life was from his very conception up to his burial. As biblical scholars comment, the narration of Jesus's temptations depicts the summary of the entire thirty-three-year deserted life-experience of Jesus.

Unquestionably, no human is exempted from being tempted by the evil forces either to ignore doing good or to surrender to perform evil. Surprisingly, Jesus, the Son of God, experienced it. The author of Letter to the Hebrews describes Jesus as *"one who has similarly been tested in every way, yet without sin"* (Heb. 5:15b). We all would be wondering how Jesus could go through the devil's temptations without committing any sin. In other words, how could he succeed in his spiritual battle?

The practical and realistic answer is found in Luke's portrayal of Jesus's victory over those temptations posed by the devil. The first matter in this regard is to be well understood. Every Tom, Dick, and Harry is not commonly taken into the swirl of temptations that Jesus underwent. Only those who are filled, shaped, molded, and moved by the Spirit as Jesus was led—only these encounter such hectic temptations. Secondly, if we observe the event attentively, we find Jesus was tempted only at the end of, and not during, his spiritual accomplishment of "forty days and forty nights" fasting for attempting to attain an intimate ecstatic relationship with his God. From this, we are clearly told most of the temptations of the devil take their express-delivery of forbidden apples to boost the human pride, self-satisfaction, and full freedom to exercise even legitimately human creative power against the Creator. This is the truth we discover in Jesus's spiritual warfare with the devil.

Humans are already led by their Creator to toddle, to walk, to run, and to float over or swim against the current of life in this earth. Besides, being reborn in Christ as his disciples, most of us are again and again led by his Spirit to various deserted situations of life. Unquestionably, whenever we try our best to relate ourselves to God intensely through our spiritual exercises of prayer, penance, fasting, and sharing, we feel happy with Jesus. We did our best, and spiritually, God guarantees we are his beloved sons and daughters. It is then, then only starts all the problems, the hell of temptations let loose as Jesus experienced.

What should we do to win over the temptations? The one and only suggestion offered to us is to hold on to a persistent faith in God. We should first make sure we have integrated all our torn and broken pieces of life—the different dimensions of life and the various creatures, creations, and especially diverse human beings we are related to. To choose our life priorities and lead a balanced life is very much based on the faith we place on the Word of God. The Word and the world must be integrated; the body and soul, the flesh and the spirit, must be united as it has been with Jesus's Incarnation. And that must be possibly done only we place all those pieces to the whole-we name God. He is the past, the present, and future; he is the beginning, the middle, and the end; he is the giver and gifts as well.

Secondly, this God of ours must be heard and believed in his spoken, written words. Thirdly, and very importantly, he must be encountered fully and really by the mutual "agape" we share with him and his fellow men. Merely celebrating this love once a year as Valentine's Day won't help us much in this regard. Our heart and mind and soul must be engaged every moment of our lives in that spirit of love.

We notice this strategy applied by Jesus not to succumb to satanic temptations. Like him, not only should we memorize and speak out God's Word, but we should also imbibe their spirit and truth within us as our blood and bones. Jesus became a model for us on how to use the Word of God on our journey, our day-to-day life. Our life is like a symphonic orchestra; "it is neither bland unison nor harsh cacophony, but a gloriously dramatic polyphony." Such a polyphonic integration in balance can happen only by the Word of God. If this miracle happens in all our spiritual exercises or religious rituals and observances, then certainly we will overcome any temptation.

THIRTEENTH WEEKEND

Second Lenten Sunday
The "Hilltop Experiences"

About eight days after he said this, he took Peter, John, and James and went up the mountain to pray. While he was praying, his face changed in appearance, and his clothing became dazzling white . . . Peter and his companions had been overcome by sleep, but becoming fully awake, they saw his glory . . . Peter said to Jesus, "Master, it is good that we are here . . ."

(Luke 9:28–36)

The French mathematician and philosopher Blaise Pascal, who lived over three hundred years ago—in the closing years of his life, struggling with his own issues of faith and understanding—wrote: "In faith there is enough light for those who want to believe, and enough shadow to blind those who don't."

We plan out our schedule—our starting, proceeding, and ending of our enterprises and engagements. Almost, we feel sure we have in our fingertips a beautiful plan of action for life. The chain of our actions—though many times they breed some other reactions as side effects—has ultimately some purpose and goal to be achieved. Even though we are aware that there will be shortcomings, failures, and losses and blunders and dark days in life, still we try to hide or ignore it and plan for 100 percent full happiness and contentment.

Very strangely, in this plan of actions, we don't want to include the "ultimate thing": our death and what follows up, namely, eternity. This is how Peter, James, and John pretend themselves when they had an ecstatic experience on a hilltop. They did not want it to end. They didn't want this special touch of heaven, this transformation or transfiguration of the Lord, this visit by Moses and Elijah. None of this—they didn't want any of it to end. "Let's put up tents," they said. "Let's hold on to this moment," they meant. But it had to end. It all had to end because the plan had to take place, and they were just mere, small ultimate things symbolically foretelling what was to come: the "Ultimate Thing."

Living with longing and describing about this Ultimate Thing very enthusiastically, Jesus's disciples, like Paul, wholeheartedly were convinced that *"he will change our lowly body to conform with his glorified body by the power that enables him also to bring all things into subjection to himself"* (Phil. 3:21). Our forbearers, like Abraham, were awesome role models for hoping of this Ultimate Thing. They happily lived their daily life, filled with accidents and incidents, with faith in the realization of what is hoped for and evidence of things not seen. Abraham, for example, set out boldly from his native place to a strange land only in the faith and hope he possessed within his heart; he too walked by faith throughout his life despite all the odds and hurdles that upset him and his family. And so with all the genuine disciples of Jesus in the past and at present as well.

The main source of this amazing life of faith and hope has been, as we read in the lives of biblical heroes and heroines, nothing but the "split-second" encounter with the striking presence of God. The supreme Divine meets with the earthly human spirit in timeless time. To walk in the valley of darkness, this spiritual lightning from the sky to the earth helps the humans and strengthens them to go a long way to reach their Promised Land. The event of transfiguration we meditate on today, which is fondly called the "hilltop experience," is one among those encounters.

It is simply a heavenly encounter with the Supreme Being. In this encounter with God, a human spirit is elevated, connected, related, and intimately present with their Creator, the Heavenly Father. God speaks and the human spirit listens. During this experience, humans lose themselves but gain God. They become nobody but everybody; they are nowhere but everywhere. They see not one thing but everything; they lose something of them but gain everything of them. They don't care about themselves—rather, they focus only on God. When a human spirit comes across such a heavenly experience, it feels it is trapped and intoxicated. Everybody who enters into this experience withdraws from the self-holding and is completely possessed by the Divine.

This breathtaking experience with God can be only a split second, simply a sparkle like that of a lightning strike. Every child from Adam to the newly born baby this day is entitled to this experience. Many people in human history have benefitted by it. Such was the vision all the disciples of Jesus held in their inner minds, particularly when they underwent persecution and death. They too attested to it and proclaimed it joyfully in dungeon and fire.

Besides many good gifts, Jesus's main purpose of coming down from heaven is just to show the way for his disciples to encounter the Divine as often as possible. He too showed us an example for how to get these hilltop experiences. Prayer time and suffering time are the apt occasions to enjoy these spiritual experiences with God. Such moments can keep us going for a long time.

FOURTEENTH WEEKEND

Third Lenten Sunday
Our God Is "Two-in-One"

And he told them this parable: "There once was a person who had a fig tree planted in his orchard, and when he came in search of fruit on it but found none, he said to the gardener, 'For three years now I have come in search of fruit on this fig tree but have found none. [So] cut it down. Why should it exhaust the soil?' He said to him in reply, 'Sir, leave it for this year also, and I shall cultivate the ground around it and fertilize it; it may bear fruit in the future. If not, you can cut it down.'"

(Luke 13:6–9)

Kindly don't misunderstand that I am disowning my faith in the dogma of Trinity. I firmly uphold my Christian Creed of "God in Three Persons." In this meditation, I want to throw some light on another dimension of our God spelt out throughout the Bible, which reiterates that God is both just and compassionate as well. In a very eminent way, the Gospel passage we have selected for today's meditation proclaims this "three-in-one" personality of God.

This fact is plainly brought out by a tiny parable of Jesus, the Grand Teacher. In the story, besides the fig tree representing humans, there are two persons debating with each other about the fate of the fig tree that has not yielded any fruit as it was designed. These two persons symbolize vividly the two characters of God. The owner of the orchard symbolizes the just side of God, and the gardener epitomizes his second side of being compassionate and patient. Ultimately, the winner is the compassionate character of God.

Jesus, as we know throughout his life, was never exhausted in emphasizing the compassionate dimension of God's character. He has so many sayings and parables to portray this truth. In his story of the fig tree, he expresses the eternal patience of God with his humans, waiting and waiting, in their pathway of life for their conversion from sinfulness. The merciful God is patient and gives everyone a chance. At the same time, Jesus never missed to remind his contemporaries the just side of God's nature by explaining the historical accidents and calamities that occurred at his time as well as in biblical history (Luke 13:1–5). As a matter of fact, Jesus insists how God's compassion and mercy can wear out because he is just, and he will punish the sinners.

Though Gospel writers list many conditions to follow Jesus as his disciples, they underscore the effective strategy of maintaining our discipleship with Jesus in order to claim our rewards from God is nothing but "to be just as the Heavenly Father is just" and "to be merciful as the Almighty is merciful." There is no alternate way to attain the heavenly crown for all that we accomplish as Jesus's disciples. In this regard, Paul is our role model. In his Letters, we perceive how awesomely he intertwines God's resolute justice and his enduring mercy as well.

Paul, in his First Letter to the Corinthians, points out how God could not tolerate the disobedience and indifference of human beings, especially his chosen ones. He writes that our merciful God—though he did so many miraculous deeds for the life, freedom, and happiness of his people—was not pleased with most of them and, therefore, struck them down in the desert; he even destroyed them all because of their evil deeds. God thus showed his nature of being just. At the same time, Paul also adds that the same God, out of compassion, had led his people through the saving waters and given them manna to eat, even though many failed to respond to his love and perished (1 Cor. 10:1–12).

Our God, whom we worship, is both compassionate and just as well. As a holy and heavenly Father, his only dream is that all his human children should attain their destiny. An entire lifetime is given to each of us to bear fruits to carry with us to eternal life. At the same time, God knows we—on our way to eternity—fail, stumble, fall, faint, detour, and deviate due to our human weakness, sinfulness, ignorance, perverted freedom, and pride. With deep concern for us, God waits for our complete winning. In compassion, he is patiently waiting for our conversion and sanctification. He gives us freedom to choose to rise up and to return to him; he too gives a long rope and allows us to prolong our indifference, coldness, and carelessness; and he even permits us to go to hit the bottom. It is left to us either to catch the same rope and climb up from the pit or to use the same rope to hang and ruin ourselves. He uses the signs of the time to bring us back to our right senses and to view our life as it is. These signs are those natural calamities, disasters happening around us, other people's sickness, death, and especially all the evil things that occur to us in our private and family life. God waits for our conversion. This is God's justice-oriented compassion. The justice of God always makes itself felt; but to us, it sometimes appears unjust!

FIFTEENTH WEEKEND

Fourth Lenten Sunday
Celebrate Life with God in Gusto

The tax collectors and sinners were all drawing near to listen to him, but the Pharisees and scribes began to complain, saying, "This man welcomes sinners and eats with them." So to them he addressed this parable . . . Then the celebration began . . . Now the older son had been out in the field and, on his way back, as he neared the house, he heard the sound of music and dancing . . . He became angry, and when he refused to enter the house, his father came out and pleaded with him. He said to his father in reply, "Look, all these years I served you and not once did I disobey your orders; yet you never gave me even a young goat to feast on with my friends. But when your son returns who swallowed up your property with prostitutes, for him you slaughter the fattened calf." He said to him, "My son, you are here with me always; everything I have is yours. But now we must celebrate and rejoice, because your brother was dead and has come to life again; he was lost and has been found."

(Luke 15:1–3, 11–32)

One of the God-given pleasures we can legitimately indulge in is eating and drinking. Especially if it is a banquet with sumptuous meals and delicious selective drinks, our hearts are enthralled. Such a pleasure trip turns out to be very limited and sometimes very dangerous to our health too. But the banquet for which God invites us daily to enjoy is something unique that is healthy, ever tasty, and never comes to an end. It is nothing but the banquet of God's mercy, love, compassion, and forgiveness.

It is amazing to read in the Bible how God spends not only his timeless time in his heavenly abode but also his "Emmanuelic" time among humans. Jesus very well portrays through his parables that God's one and only preoccupation is celebrating joyfully—preparing sumptuous meals of joy, peace, and forgiveness and inviting and waiting for and waiting on as well all his human creatures at his table. That is what we meditate on today with the Gospel sharing of Luke 15. The only source of enjoyment in God's celebration is, above all, the times when we receive the forgiveness and thus a warm welcome ceremony from the Lord. During those moments, our hearts beat with David's hymn: *"The Lord is the redeemer of the souls of his servants; and none are condemned who take refuge in him"* (Ps. 34:23). Our lips mutter frequently, "My God has forgiven me and accepted me into his banquet chamber." It is this thought and conviction that makes us rejoice and celebrate every minute joyfully as the younger prodigal son did.

Unfortunately, there are too many among us who lose—like the elder son—such noble moments as Jesus indicates in his parable. The only problem with such "elder sons" is they easily forget the fact that they too are still sinners like their younger brothers. Every human being is a sinner.

Henri Nouwen beautifully described it in writing: "We are all handicapped; some are more visibly handicapped than others." Whether our sins are more visible like those of the younger son or more hidden like those of the elder son, the message for us today is that we all need to repent and return to the Father's house. As the younger son does, so the elder son needs to turn back from anger and resentment and learn to share the house with the apparently undeserving younger brother.

He was indeed a very nice young man, always with his beliefs and values. But he could not enjoy as much happiness as his younger brother at the father's banquet. Even though he was grown up physically, he was yet underdeveloped in his emotions and spirit. There are too many among us who feel like the elder son, who are complacent in what we hold in life today. We are content with what we perform as religious observances, but we never have time to look into how our relationship stands with God. We may apparently stay inside the house of the Father but, very sadly, like the elder son, they would be far distant, away from the heart of the Father.

So today, God speaks to us: "Are you far away from my heart of forgiveness and compassion though you are inside my home? You should celebrate the life I gave you." He too, with his brokenhearted fatherliness, tells us through David: *"Oh, that today you would hear his voice; do not harden your hearts . . . your ancestors tested me; they tried me though they had seen my works. Forty years I loathed that generation; I said: 'This people's heart goes astray; they do not know my ways.' Therefore I swore in my anger: 'They shall never enter my rest.'"* (Ps. 95:7–11)

Fifth Lenten Sunday
The Lord Has Done Great Things for Us

Then the scribes and the Pharisees brought a woman who had been caught in adultery and made her stand in the middle. They said to him, "Teacher, this woman was caught in the very act of committing adultery . . . Jesus bent down and began to write on the ground with his finger. But when they continued asking him, he straightened up and said to them, "Let the one among you who is without sin be the first to throw a stone at her" . . . And in response, they went away one by one, beginning with the elders . . . Then Jesus straightened up and said to her, "Woman, where are they? Has no one condemned you?" She replied, "No one, sir." Then Jesus said, "Neither do I condemn you. Go, and from now on do not sin anymore."

(John 8:3–11)

We hear about studies in business management, crisis management, life management, time management, family management, and so on. There are thousands of books and research works sold out in market to learn the theories about them. Have you ever heard of "sin management"? While there are too many courses conducted in hundreds of colleges and universities, there is only one university and one and only textbook for learning the theories and principles of sin management. Church is the one university, and the Bible is the one and only textbook. The scriptural passage we meditate on this weekend instructs us in managing our sins.

Being very clever creatures as we are, there are some natural tactics we usually apply to manage our sinfulness. As soon as we come to our senses regarding our committing sin, our inner peace is disturbed. We are hurt and therefore act or react against this situation, not being able to manage the sinfulness in a productive way. In scrupulosity, we begin to feel always guilty; or in frozen complacency, our naughty brain makes us insensitive to the sins' horror. Many of us distract ourselves from the conscience-prick by various hurry-burry "jollyhood" lifestyles or drifting away from faith and religion with unprecedented justifications. We too have seen some others developing a stony heart and hardheadedness; and we throw stones at others, thus soothing their own consciences.

Scriptures teach us first the horrendous results of human sins. Sin is some kind of attitude and deed that goes against God's love, against our own human spirit, against the wholistic truth, and against our relationship with other human beings. In addition, the Word of God teaches us also how to manage that horrible aftermath of sinning. God's "sin management" theory, according to scriptures, is:

The more we feel guilty, the nearer we go to God—who loves sinners though he hates sin. He, as Father, hugs us immediately as the prodigal's father did to his younger son at his return. Secondly, when we come to our senses and confess our sinfulness, we must think not about our own ugly past. *"Remember not the events of the past, the things of long ago consider not. See, I am doing something new!"* (Isa. 43:18–19). As some writers put it, "God has a very bad memory." No matter how many times the Israelites abandoned their God, no matter how many times they became "stiff-necked" and refused to do his will, he always came to call them back. In the whole of the New Testament, we see God—in the person of Jesus—calling his sinful people to be converted, to put their whole trust in the message he brings and to follow his way as the "way of truth and life."

We also must confess more the marvelous deeds of God. This is what all converted, confessed, and pardoned sinners like Paul did and do. Paul writes: *"Just one thing: forgetting what lies behind but straining forward to what lies ahead, I continue my pursuit toward the goal, the prize of God's upward calling, in Christ Jesus"* (Phil. 3:13–14). Thirdly, we must not behave as if we have received a cheap grace. We must do something proactively, confessing not merely by words but by deeds of charities. Above all, we should remove completely the stones in our spirit and forgive others. In the biblical story we meditate on this weekend, we see many sinners around Jesus: a woman and a group of Pharisees and scribes. They represent all of us. Usually, humans sin in two ways. As the woman caught in adultery, we hurt God and others by indulging our desires at their expense; also, as the Pharisees and scribes, we hurt others by setting ourselves up as superior to and esteem ourselves better than them as well.

If we had been there that day, what would we have done? Would we have condemned the guilty woman too? Even during the past week, how many people have we condemned in our hearts or in our words? Are we regular readers of newspapers or watchers of TV programs that delight in rubbishing people and destroying their lives? How many people have we ourselves passed judgment on? On the other hand, to how many have we extended a hand of love and compassion?

When we begin to manage our sinfulness in the light of Jesus's Gospel theory, we will experience a restful life going through green pastures. And we will ceaselessly sing joyfully with King David, who was another typical sinner of our kind: *"The Lord has done great things for us; we are filled with joy"* (Ps. 126).

Palm Sunday
The Passionate Passion of the Lord

> *Do nothing out of selfishness or out of vainglory; rather, humbly regard others as more important than yourselves, each looking out not for his own interests, but [also] everyone for those of others. Have among yourselves the same attitude that is also yours in Christ Jesus, who, though he was in the form of God, did not regard equality with God something to be grasped. Rather, he emptied himself, taking the form of a slave, coming in human likeness; and found human in appearance, he humbled himself, becoming obedient to death, even death on a cross. Because of this, God greatly exalted him . . . (Phil. 2:3–11)*

As Jesus was entering Jerusalem to meet his climactic end of physical life, he got a warm and glorious welcome from his followers, beneficiaries, and onlookers. With pride and joy, all the Gospel writers add this event as the introduction to their "passion narratives." Spreading their cloaks and strewing leafy branches on the road Jesus was riding, waving palm branches as a sign of jubilation and victory, a large crowd of disciples and common people in Jerusalem preceded him. And those following kept crying out and saying, "Hosanna to the Son of David; blessed is he who comes in the name of the Lord."

Undoubtedly, while Jesus accepted this warm welcome, he never put his heart into it—because firstly, he knew what was in humans! Secondly, he was fully aware of where his Father, together with this crowd, was taking him: to the slaughterhouse! His entire preoccupation was how to surrender himself willingly, humbly, patiently, and joyfully to the passion and death he would be enduring. He certainly didn't want the passion he possessed throughout his life from conception to the final days ever to be extinguished. He was filled with emotions of longing and craving to fulfill the will of his Father and a passion for performing an eternal sacrifice for the future of humanity, his brothers and sisters.

We humans are aware of our own humanness. When we are entangled with an immense passion for some earthly things, for some living creatures, or for some worldly ambitions, we forget anything about ourselves. We go ahead with full will and emotions to accomplish or to covet what we desire. This is what we encounter in Jesus regarding his commitment to his Father, to whom he promised as he entered into this world: *"Behold, I come to do your Will, O God."* This sort of "journey of passion" had not started just this Sunday, but as he came into the world from heaven. Paul reminds us today how the Son of God emptied himself, came down to the earth, stripped of his glory, took the form of a slave, and was ready to undergo any death, even death on a cross. Jesus's passion to fulfill totally the desire of his Father was urging him to move forward.

In this journey of passion, Jesus's one and only focus was to bring spiritual liberation and renewal to humans.

When he was greeted by the people, he felt sorry for them because not all of them were well aware of what exactly he was engaged in. Surely, they expected a Messiah as a big warrior who would support them in their political, social, and other earthly needs. Unfortunately, he did not give any glimpse for such identity while he was traveling through Palestine for three years. His teachings were always centered on love, forgiveness, peace, patience, and Spirit and Truth. When they tried once to make him a king, he drifted away. They were waiting for an opportune time.

They believed this Sunday, as he entered Jerusalem visibly, he would demonstrate his real identity of his worldly power, glory, and tenacity. But everything happened opposite to their dreams. They were disappointed completely with him as they observed what went on during this week. Their hearts were very fickle, so they turned against him and shouted while he was before Pilate, "Away with him!" However, the passion in Jesus never faded away. He stood his ground and went through the passion events. This is how we got Jesus as a world leader and Savior.

Let us appreciate him and accept him as our leader. Let us follow him wherever he takes us. Let us be bold enough to say "*Come, let us go and die with him.*" Let us be passionate about the passion of the Lord so that we too can be immerged into that bleeding passion to walk the walk of obedience and to lift up the world around us as God's kingdom.

Easter Sunday
This Is the Day the Lord Has
Made; Let Us Rejoice in It

You know . . . what has happened all over Judea, beginning in Galilee after the baptism that John preached; God anointed Jesus of Nazareth with the Holy Spirit and power. He went about doing good and healing all those oppressed by the devil, for God was with him. We are witnesses of all that he did both in the country of the Jews and (in) Jerusalem. They put him to death by hanging him on a tree. This man God raised (on) the third day and granted that he be visible, not to all the people, but to us, the witnesses chosen by God in advance, who ate and drank with him after he rose from the dead. He commissioned us to preach to the people and testify that he is the one appointed by God as judge of the living and the dead. To him all the prophets bear witness, that everyone who believes in him will receive forgiveness of sins through his name." (Acts 10:36–43)

God will survive even without us, but we cannot survive without him. To survive with God is what we call religion or church. In life, there are a thousand and one unsolved mysteries, millions of unresolved bad times, and incalculable unfulfilled dreams. The world seems as dark as any of the other centuries. This human experience of darkness and gloominess about life is so universal that one humorous person noted: "Life is just one damn thing after another."

Then how do we survive through this grim darkness? It is all by stories, fantasies, fairy tales, daydreams, and memories of the past. Those stories are not only read or heard but also remembered, believed, and celebrated. That is what a religion is all about, and so is our church. The story of the Resurrection is one among many. However, the Resurrection story is not meant to be just remembered, believed, and celebrated. The Easter story is not at all to be listed in the top ten stories like Santa's. It is a story not just to be told or to be pretended, but it is to be lived and experienced.

Our New Testament books proclaim this fact of Christianity. They all enumerate what went before and came after the Resurrection of Jesus. Who was this Jesus before he was resurrected? We read Peter preaching that this risen Jesus was an ordinary human, full of God's Spirit, who went through the challenges of his individual life but never drifted away from the higher ideals he imposed to himself for his life-journey. We can even say that as he was dying and being buried, his spirit would have continued to whisper with hope and conviction in his "beyondness" with the Psalmist's words: *"I shall not die but live and declare the deeds of the Lord. The Lord chastised me harshly, but did not hand me over to death. The stone the builders rejected has become the cornerstone"* (Ps. 118).

As for the aftermath results of "resurrection," we read in the Bible that whoever visited or reflected over the empty tomb where Jesus had been buried and believed that his resurrection was a true but heavenly event in human history—they were historically empowered, renewed, rejuvenated, and began like freaks witnessing to this resurrected human being. The only testimony they submitted was "We have encountered the resurrected Lord; he urged us to live and preach his Gospel of Mercy and Joy."

Paul, one among those "freaks" of Jesus, reiterates in all his Letters the real effects of Jesus's resurrection. According to him, if it is true that we have been resurrected by the belief in the risen Jesus, the only sign for such a miracle is nothing but the living of our daily life. *"If then you were raised with Christ, seek what is above, where Christ is seated at the right hand of God. Think of what is above, not of what is on earth. For you have died, and your life is hidden with Christ in God. When Christ your life appears, then you too will appear with him in glory"* (Col. 3:1–4).

In the midst of so many debates going on for and against Jesus's resurrection, the main source for present-day disciples' belief in it is what they personally experience as its "aftermath effects." Our individual and personal experience of Jesus alive is the unended gospel of Jesus and the unfinished task of Jesus. The Resurrection story is not at all for being proved by an outsider or any outside technique or strategy. It is to be lived and experienced by each and every one of us. We are that team, that family, that community of which every member has been experiencing the resurrected Lord in our daily lives. If what we say about the resurrection of Jesus to others, especially to our young ones, had not been accepted and believed, it is because we ourselves have not gotten that experience of Jesus resurrected in our lives. The story of the Resurrection is not like that of Santa's. The Santa story can be pretended, faked—but not the resurrected Lord.

NINETEENTH WEEKEND

Second Easter Sunday
The Unbroken Chain Effect of Resurrection

> *Thomas, called Didymus, one of the Twelve, was not with them when Jesus came . . . But he said to them, "Unless I see the mark of the nails in his hands and put my finger into the nailmarks and put my hand into his side, I will not believe . . ." Jesus came, although the doors were locked, and stood in their midst and said, "Peace be with you." Then he said to Thomas, "Put your finger here and see my hands, and bring your hand and put it into my side, and do not be unbelieving, but believe." Thomas answered and said to him, "My Lord and my God!" Jesus said to him, "Have you come to believe because you have seen me? Blessed are those who have not seen and have believed."*
>
> (John 20:24–29)

We hear the risen Lord expressing his desire to his disciples as he showed himself to Thomas that *"blessed are those who have not seen and have believed."* Let us ponder over what was in his mind with his own sayings and actions underlined in the New Testament books. Unquestionably, with Paul, we profess that "we walk by faith and not by sight." But many critics contend that it impossible to believe God the invisible, and it is either fake or superstitious. We agree with our faith critics that we normally recognize, accept, and believe in ourselves, in others, and in other things by the process of hearing, seeing, touching, smelling, and tasting.

Generally, in the context of religions, we deal with the supernatural and spiritual beings—namely, God, saints, angels, devils, and the dead too. In Christianity alone, we believe—besides God and other spiritual beings—a person called Jesus of Nazareth, who was dead and buried but alive today. We believe in the risen Jesus exactly as John writes about his vision in the Book of Revelation: *"I am the first and the last, the one who lives. Once I was dead, but now I am alive forever and ever. I hold the keys to death and the netherworld."* We uncompromisingly believe that the same Jesus is alive in the church, in its authority, in its worship, in its sacraments, and in its preaching.

In this encounter of believing in Jesus alive, can our sensory acts of hearing, seeing, smelling, tasting, and touching precede? This is a valid question and a legitimate normal demand of any human being, as with Thomas: *"Unless I see and touch, I will not believe."* We should know Thomas was not the only person in the apostles' team who saw and believed Jesus. We read in the Gospels how John and others ran to the empty tomb, saw the linen, and believed. All the apostles saw the resurrected Lord, ate with him, spoke with him, heard him speak, and believed. Even Paul, after seeing Jesus persecuted in one of his visions, believed in him. This is why as John, every apostle and even other disciples could boldly proclaim Jesus's Gospel, stating: *". . . for the life* (Jesus) *was made visible; we have seen it and testify to it and proclaim to you the eternal life that was with the Father and was made visible to us what we have seen and heard we proclaim now to you"* (1 John

1:2–3). Paul, therefore, could state: *"For how can people believe in him of whom they have not heard?"* (Rom. 10:14).

So "believing by seeing" has been a normal course or process of believing in Jesus alive. Yet what did Jesus mean telling Thomas that "not seeing but believing" is better? What the Lord said was not meant to ignore or deny the normal and legitimate process of believing. Rather, he wanted his disciples to live and move in the realm of his Spirit. He made us understand that the continuity of his mission in this world would be maintained by his Spirit, and he wanted us to contact him in the spiritual way. He is not physically present as Jesus of Nazareth, even with his resurrected body as he appeared to his disciples. He wanted us to see him spiritually in his physical absence and commit ourselves to his values. This is why he breathed on them and said, "Receive the Spirit."

Let us remember here what Paul says regarding our Christian life in the Spirit: *"Now the natural person does not accept what pertains to the Spirit of God, for to him it is foolishness, and he cannot understand it, because it is judged spiritually"* (1 Cor. 2:14).

When we are moving in his Spirit and commit to Jesus—our hands, legs, eyes as his own—those who hear us, those who see us, those who touch us actually hear, see, and touch the resurrected Jesus of Nazareth! This is how Jesus's mission has been continued for the past two millennia, and it is going to be so through the third millennium too. The early Christians did not see Jesus, yet they saw and heard and touched Jesus alive in the lives and actions of the early disciples and believed and lived as if Jesus was alive. *"Many signs and wonders were done among the people at the hands of the apostles . . . Yet more than ever, believers in the Lord, great numbers of men and women, were added to them."* This awful story continues even to this day. We see, hear, and touch the risen Lord in the lives and performances of Spirit-filled disciples moving around the globe. Let us join the club of those miracle workers!

Third Easter Sunday
The Measure with Which You Measure Will Be Measured Unto You

When they had finished breakfast, Jesus said to Simon Peter, "Simon, son of John, do you love me more than these?" He said to him, "Yes, Lord, you know that I love you." He said to him, "Feed my lambs." He then said to him a second time, "Simon, son of John, do you love me?" He said to him, "Yes, Lord, you know that I love you." He said to him, "Tend my sheep." He said to him the third time, "Simon, son of John, do you love me?" Peter was distressed that he had said to him a third time, "Do you love me?" and he said to him, "Lord, you know everything; you know that I love you." Jesus said to him, "Feed my sheep."

(John 21:15–19)

Unquestionably, we, the disciples of Jesus, share the power and authority from our Master. Because we believe his promises, all his true believers certainly get a glimpse. They see him, they speak with him, they touch him, and they walk with him as a living and loving friend. These are not just stories like Hollywood Superman movies; rather, they are real and authentic life experiences of millions of Jesus's disciples over the centuries. This is why so many things are peculiar and sometimes unthinkable; they speak and perform with a unique authority and power. And they claim this exceptional authority is derived from that Jesus who is alive.

In the Gospel passage we meditate on this weekend, we see how the disciples of Jesus encountered his power and authority after his resurrection. While the human disciples were frustrated with their limitations and inabilities in their labor of fishing, with the power of the risen Lord, they succeeded—not just in what they wanted but more than what they expected. The Gospels prove that Jesus, both while he was in his physical body and in his resurrected form as well, revealed very peculiar authority and power in his words and deeds. This is why the people and higher authorities during his time were wondering about the authority with which he spoke and did miracles. His disciples witnessed, within his three years of public life, his marvelous power and authority. Hence, even when he was out of their sight, they continued to state publicly and proudly that their Teacher was a "Superman" with all power and authority. Though he seemed like a voiceless lamb to be easily mistreated, they never ceased to proclaim: *"To the One seated on the throne, and to the Lamb, be praise and honor, glory and might, forever and ever!"* (Rev. 5:13)

We know our Master entrusted the same power and authority when he promised us, saying: *"All power in heaven and on earth has been given to me. Go therefore and make disciples of all nations, baptizing them in the name of the Father, and of the Son, and of the Holy Spirit, teaching them to observe all that I commanded you. And behold, I am with you always, until the end of age"* (Matt. 28:18–20). He too confirmed that we would receive his Spirit of power and authority with which we can do all things, even greater than he did. Jesus alive, once he befriends us, he grants—rather, his Spirit starts integrating with our human spirit, and our whole life perspective, worldview, and attitudes change. We begin to live in a totally different realm of life. People around us watch and find out a certain strangeness about our behavior, our way of going through life's ordinary and extraordinary events with certain tenacious authority.

While we feel very happy and proud about such an amazing dealing of the risen Lord with us, there are times when almost all of us begin to misuse or abuse the delegated power bestowed by our Master. History and each one's conscience testify to it. We forget to be very careful in discerning that authority formed in us, truly and genuinely generated from the risen Lord. With lack of such discerning, many of us, as we climb up the ladder of power and authority, as with many religious leaders, perpetuate bloody terrorism with crazy religious convictions. How do we find out if the power and authority we hold is truly from the risen Lord or merely from out of our own IQ, shrewd diplomacy, and political manipulating?

Good Peter and others of his company were typical humans, as we are all natural-born connivers. Hence, the risen Lord encounters us through Peter in an incident that happened at the seashore of Tiberias. By asking Peter three times whether he loved him more than others, Jesus wanted not only to confirm for himself that Peter did love him before he confirmed his handing over to Peter his personal and functional authority, but also mainly to emphasize to Peter and all of his disciples that our authority must start with love and end with service. Love and service are the only yardstick with which we can measure the source of personal authority. Sadly, according to that criterion, most of our words and actions fall short of their credibility. So today, let us claim the Lord's presence in our midst. In order to make sure our inner power is that of the risen Lord, let us be attentive—namely, to fight the good fight, to love Jesus, to hunger for him, and from time to time, check with our own authority-based actions, whether they are emerging out of love for Jesus alive and whether they are producing services to others and the universe as the Master wills.

TWENTY-FIRST WEEKEND

Fourth Easter Sunday
The True Sheep Can Become Shepherds of the Good Shepherd

These are the ones who have survived the time of great distress; they have washed their robes and made them white in the blood of the Lamb. For this reason, they stand before God's throne and worship him day and night in his temple. The one who sits on the throne will shelter them. They will not hunger or thirst anymore, nor will the sun or any heat strike them. For the Lamb who is in the center of the throne will shepherd them and lead them to springs of life-giving water, and God will wipe away every tear from their eyes.
(Rev. 7:14b–17)

We, the disciples of Jesus, never cease to address our Master as the "Good Shepherd." We should know that this famous Shepherd, who was given by the Heavenly Father such a glorious role of shepherding us, first was a hidden, small, innocent, and meek Lamb of God. He was an obedient child of God. Jesus was a sheep to his Father, who was his Shepherd. Following little shepherd David, Jesus would have been singing every day, *"The Lord is my Shepherd. I shall want nothing."* He behaved as a lamb to his Father. He was slain like a lamb to do the will of his Father. His will and his Father's will were

78

so tuned up with the same rhythm that he could bravely state: *"I and my Father are one."* As John the Baptizer named him the "Lamb of God," Jesus became a scapegoat and was slaughtered for the sake of his Father's creative and redemptive plan to be fulfilled. John the Evangelist therefore could see him as a lamb sitting on the throne of heaven. This is the stuff with which Jesus breathed, moved, and lived as Jesus of Nazareth; and that is why God exalted him above any other name and entrusted to him the most glorious role of shepherding the sheep of his own flock.

When the same Good Shepherd planned to delegate his power of shepherding to his disciples, he primarily wanted them to behave like true sheep. He commanded them to be genuine and true sheep, recognizing him, listening to him, and following him. As they continued to humbly and faithfully follow him, they saw themselves—their weakness and strength, and their status and destiny. They boldly testified as Paul, proclaiming, *"For so the Lord has commanded us, I have made you a light to the Gentiles, that you may be an instrument of salvation to the ends of the earth."* All those disciples were following their Shepherd wherever he led them; even when they felt as if they were in a dark valley, they kept on following him till their last drop of blood poured out for the sake of their Shepherd's creative and redemptive plan to be fulfilled. They became, in history, as *"the ones who have survived the time of great distress; they have washed their robes and made them white in the blood of the Lamb."* Consequently, they were truly recognized by God as good shepherds.

Almost all of us, as we enter into adulthood (for some even earlier), long to be leaders and shepherds. Students prefer to be teachers, staff long to be bosses, laborers dream to be masters, and youngsters love to be elders and masters of their own destiny. There is nothing bad about all these preferences and dreams. The question is how to be climbing up or realizing such dreams? Besides, when we have climbed up to the top, how are we going to manage and maintain that position intact and productive and cool?

The only answer to this is to look at ourselves through the mirror of Jesus's personality and behavior. Jesus wants us to live and behave exactly as he did with his Father. The will of the sheep must become one with the will of the Shepherd. Otherwise, sheep remain sheep and not a shepherd in fulfilling life's responsibility of leading others.

True sheep of Jesus are to be "one with the shepherd" in spirit and in truth. They not only move around the sheepfold, are registered as his sheep in a church, and belong to his sheepfold just for baptism and burial, but they are intimately attached to the shepherd. They move and stand with him wherever he goes, run after him wherever he takes, listen to him attentively, act according to his commands, and abide in him as branches in the vine. The will of the sheep must become one with the will of the Shepherd. Otherwise, sheep remain sheep and not a shepherd in fulfilling life's responsibility of leading others.

We are sheep only to Jesus, the Good Shepherd. We are weak only before God, for we are strong warriors before Satan. We are humble followers only to the Lamb of God but courageous leaders to our children and other weaklings of the society. If we want such identity and dignity to stay within us, we have to then be true sheep of Jesus and not wolves in sheep's clothing. The more we ignore and resist our Shepherd, the less powerful, less fruitful we become. Let us therefore remain with our Good Shepherd closely and love him totally, know him intimately, and listen to him obediently to take his shepherding role in our life situations.

TWENTY-SECOND WEEKEND

Fifth Easter Sunday
"Behold, I Make All Things New"

When he had left, Jesus said, "Now is the Son of Man glorified, and God is glorified in him. If God is glorified in him, God will also glorify him in himself, and he will glorify him at once . . . I give you a new commandment: love one another. As I have loved you, so you also should love one another. This is how all will know that you are my disciples, if you have love for one another." (John 13:31–35)

The dream of a new order in personal and social life is the perennial quest of our human race. In every age, the leaders and gurus of the people promised such a new order. In their enlightenment and intelligence, they listed many strategies, tricks, norms, and mantras to realize it; but most of their tips turned out to be either unproductive or completely wrong and perverted and, in some cases, pharisaical, diplomatic, and self-centered means. Jesus too preached about this order. However, he—naming this new order as the "Kingdom of God"—proposed the strategy of achieving it, which is totally different from others.

Before Jesus was born, God promised through his prophets this human dream would be realized. Asking people to shout for joy and be glad forever in what God is creating, through Prophet Isaiah, God declared: *"See, I am creating new heavens and a new earth; the former things shall not be remembered nor come to mind"* (Isa. 65:17–18). When Jesus came, lived, died, and rose from the dead, all his disciples believed and proclaimed loudly that the promise of God has been realized in their Master. Paul exclaimed, writing about the "Jesus Effect": *"So whoever is in Christ is a new creation: the old things have passed away; behold, new things have come"* (2 Cor. 5:17). And John, whom Jesus exclusively loved, saw a vision about this "New Order" fact. He not only saw a new heaven and a new earth, where the former heaven and the former earth had passed away, and the sea was no more; but also he heard the Lamb, Jesus, sitting on his heavenly throne, saying, *"Behold, I make all things new"* (Rev. 21:1–5).

Jesus proposed the one and only means to achieve his and our dream of a New Order. That strategy, in the light of the Spirit and the scriptures, we can very well underscore is nothing but letting our individual human life being led, renewed, and wheeled around by love. When he arrived in the earth, so many versions about the idea of love were floating in the globe. He compiled all of them but added not a twist but eternally graded nuance to them. This is what we meditate on this weekend. At his Last Supper, he stated it very loudly: *"As I have loved you, so you also should love one another."*

The love Jesus demanded from his followers is one that would get the source and energy from the awesome love that has been demonstrated by God the Father and significantly in his Son, Jesus. The characteristics of the love he proposed were three: First, our love should be in the agape style of God. The word *agape* means "the unlimited, pure love of God." Jesus's human love was fully centered on God and his love. As his Father God, Jesus expected us to be gracious and merciful, slow to anger, and of great kindness—to be good to all and compassionate.

Secondly, Jesus wanted us to love others only for others, and not for any reciprocation or recognition; it is purely other-centered love. There are no strings attached to it. In our love for others, Jesus expects us to recognize and accept one another as Jesus recognizes each one of us. This implies we should not draw any boundary, color, measurement, or criterion for reaching out to others. We must consider every human being as a child of God, as the sheep in his sheepfold. We need to love others with a forgiving love and with a serving and sharing love, as Jesus did and admonished.

Thirdly, Jesus's command is to love like him in detail. Each of us has to discover the best way to express our love, even in our own small ways: by choosing a kind word rather than a critical one, offering a smile or a helping hand, sending a letter to a friend, remembering someone's birthday, listening to the lonely, being patient with the impatient, or showing interest in someone else's plans. Saint Theresa of Child Jesus, who is fondly called the Little Flower, points out this truth in her autobiography, writing: "Only performing little things for my beloved Jesus, I gain his love."

Church history testifies clearly how exemplary so many disciples and holy men and women were in fulfilling the love commandment of Jesus. Once they were caught up by the fire of Jesus's true love, they were on their way to proclaim that new love, that new faith, that new order, and that new life in Jesus. Jesus's teaching about love is very inventive. And it is that inventive love that he makes the heart of our faith and our life. If we only had a bit of love like that, we could make ourselves and our world all new.

TWENTY-THIRD WEEKEND

Sixth Easter Sunday
A Church within and without the Church

> *He took me in spirit to a great, high mountain and showed me the holy city Jerusalem coming down out of heaven from God . . . I saw no temple in the city, for its temple is the Lord God Almighty and the Lamb. The city had no need of sun or moon to shine on it, for the glory of God gave it light, and its lamp was the Lamb.*
>
> (Rev. 21:10–14, 22–23)

One day, as I was browsing Internet blogs, I came across "The Cyber Hymnal" site in which a hymn written and composed by Kent E. Schneider was posted. It started with the verse: "There's a church within us, O Lord; not a building, but a soul; not a portion but a whole; there's a church within us, O Lord." That offered me an inspiration for this weekend's meditation. There is a church within—or even without—the church. Augustine, many centuries back, already verbalized this amazing twofold aspect of the church. He termed them "the visible" and "the invisible." What he meant was within this "one" church Jesus established, there are two realities: a visible institutional church consisting of more than two billions nominally, and there is also an invisible church that is made up of genuine believers from all ages, and who are known only to God. These members of the invisible church have actually been regenerated or quickened by the Holy Spirit, God's elect or true believers. Unbelievably, later, a good many theologians added a fact to this ecclesiology that this invisible church may include even those non-church members.

Augustine drew this debatable contention from the scriptures only, largely from the New Testament. Jesus indicated this through a parable of wheats and weeds (Matt. 13:30). He ruthlessly divided his own church members in these double categories. He separates them, as one group lisping "Lord, Lord" but not doing God's will, and the other not only saying "Lord, Lord" to him but also fulfilling what his Father expects them to do. He too underlines that at the Last Judgment, he would visibly divide his church members into two. One group, which he called goats, would be cursed; and the other, as his beloved sheep, would be blessed. The only criterion for such terrifying judgment is "observing his new commandment of love." Both Paul and Peter followed our Master's perception and wrote in their Letters: *"Set apart for the service of the gospel that God promised long ago through his prophets in the Holy Scriptures"* (Rom. 1:2). *"But you are 'a chosen race, a royal priesthood, a holy nation, a people of his own, so that you may announce the praises' of him who called you out of darkness into his wonderful light"* (1 Pet. 2:9).

These chosen ones are the Christ's disciples who make the church within the church by their intimate and committed life in, with, and through Christ. And those are the Christians who see the true church of God daily in their vision and dream as John described it in the Book of Revelation as the city where dwell those who try to wash themselves clean daily from their sinful stains in the blood of Jesus, who take the Eucharist—the body and blood of Jesus—as their daily spiritual nourishment along with God's Word, and who share their bread and savings with the community and the poor and thus try their best to be committed stewards of the Lord.

As a matter of fact, these are the people who are prone to lose peace and rest than any other people who, though residing in the same city, don't have any conscience; they have no morality and no higher values in life. As the results of their intense commitment to their Master's new commandment of love, those blessed ones undergo, actually, daily martyrdom as the Psalmist would cry out, "We are thwarted by the evil surroundings." They become overanxious, unbalanced, and restless. It is for such friendly disciples that Jesus promises: *"Do not let your hearts be troubled or afraid. Peace I leave with you; my peace I give to you. Not as the world gives do I give it to you"* (John 14:27).

So if we really belong to that elite group of Jesus, and if we desire to enjoy a lasting peace in our lives as Jesus promised, we have to uphold certain strategies in daily life. We should never lose sight of our remarkable identity as the chosen race. We should make sure that our heart and mind and body become a dwelling of the Triune God by obeying Jesus's word of love. Secondly, as the members of this spiritual church and being close friends of Jesus, we should be engaged in reforming the entire church in its physical, social, and universal dimensions. We should try our best to get rid of its false ideological principles, and then only the world will be a better place to live in. Finally, when a disagreement among us arises, which is very normal among humans, we should follow the footsteps of early Christian disciples—namely, being wise enough to submit our differences to the power of the Holy Spirit in prayer. Once we arrive at our Spirit-inspired decision, we can act with efficiency and sensitivity in the problem-solving process (Acts 15:1–29).

This is how God's chosen ones possess the true peace uninterruptedly. And if we are in that invisible club of God's chosen ones, surely, we will tell God daily as the Psalmist: *"In peace shall I sleep, Lord, in peace shall I rest: firm in the hope you have given me"* (Ps. 4:9).

Ascension Sunday
Being Empowered, We Can Triumph

> *When they had gathered together, they asked him, "Lord, are you at this time going to restore the kingdom to Israel?" He answered them, "It is not for you to know the times or seasons that the Father has established by his own authority. But you will receive power when the Holy Spirit comes upon you, and you will be my witnesses in Jerusalem, throughout Judea and Samaria, and to the ends of the earth." When he had said this, as they were looking on, he was lifted up, and a cloud took him from their sight.* (Acts 1:6–9)

Christian faith in the Paschal Mystery enacted by Jesus doesn't end with his resurrection. Scripturally, its summit is his ascension, which portrays that he finally became our triumphant Messiah-King and started reigning in glory over all creation. He gained possessing all the power and glory received from his Father for his successful life-accomplishment in this world for thirty-three years, after he had done everything that was required of him. We are so happy to hear such positive thoughts and claims about Jesus, the crucified Lord. Indeed, we feel proud of being one of the disciples and followers in this twenty-first century to such a dynamic leader in a high status.

We are happy also for another very important reason. It is for those promises he left with us before he departed from this world. He offered his followers three important promises for their "quality life." He promised that he would entrust his redemptive work to them. *"You will be my witnesses in Jerusalem, throughout Judea and Samaria, and to the ends of the earth"* (Acts). *"Go into the whole world and proclaim the gospel to every creature"* (Mark 16:15). This means he trusted them, though he *"would not trust himself to them because he knew them all, and did not need anyone to testify about human nature. He himself understood it well"* (John 2:24–25). The main reason is he loved them very much as his own siblings and was fully sure, with his intimate cooperation, they would be up to his dreams.

Another promise he gave his followers was that he would share with them his power and glory. *"I am sending the promise of my Father upon you; but stay in the city until you are clothed with power from on high"* (Luke 24:49). *"You will receive power when the Holy Spirit comes upon you"* (Acts 1:8). The power Jesus promised consists of three fruitful and resourceful elements, such as the power of faith that induces us to be firmly convinced of the presence and actions of God and his spiritual messengers; the power of hope, which is a strong vision that there is always a bright tomorrow; and the power of love through which we conduct our life and our roles with a balanced understanding of relationship, fellowship, and leadership.

History testifies his disciples realized Jesus's promise in their lives. When they got his power, they accomplished all that Jesus did and even more than he. *"These signs will accompany those who believe: in my name they will drive out demons, they will speak new languages. They will pick up serpents [with their hands], and if they drink any deadly thing, it will not harm them. They will lay hands on the sick, and they will recover"* (Mark 16:17–18).

Jesus also promised that he would never leave them orphans: *"And behold, I am with you always, until the end of the age"* (Matt. 28:20b). Up to this day, and certainly the days to come, the risen and ascended Lord stays in the church and in the hearts of his disciples and continues to work marvelous deeds, which ordinary humans can never venture and accomplish.

All these promises make us feel positive about our human life. Being a Christian is not worthless or useless. We are chosen by Christ at the time of baptism and confirmation to be his disciples. We too have accepted it. If we sincerely accept and follow Jesus as our master and leader, then all his promises will be realized in every one of us. Mainly, he will invest on us his power so that we can do marvelous work on his behalf. This power enables us to give powerful witness to Christ in our earthly life. This power is also abundantly available to us to face various sufferings and difficulties and to live our faith and gospel values. This power also helps us in our fight against the evil powers and dark forces of hell. It fills us with enlightenment and wisdom, with joy and serenity. This power assists us to repent, to forgive our enemies, and to love everyone. The million-dollar question is this: How do we appropriate this power? And how do we use it?

TWENTY-FIFTH WEEKEND

Pentecost Sunday
Powerfully Individualistic but Shamefully Disunited

> *No one can say "Jesus is Lord," except by the Holy Spirit. There are different kinds of spiritual gifts but the same Spirit; there are different forms of service but the same Lord; there are different workings but the same God who produces all of them in everyone . . . one and the same Spirit produces all of these, distributing them individually to each person as he wishes . . . For in one Spirit we were all baptized into one body, whether Jews or Greeks, slaves or free persons, and we were all given to drink of one Spirit.*
>
> (1 Cor. 12:3b–13)

We live by energy, we love energy, and we breathe energy. Our life ends when our internal system of energy ends. The most powerful forces are outside of us. We feel them, but we don't see them—and so it is with our inner energies. All these powers and energies are invisible. We see where they come from. We feel their results and know where and when they end. But we surely cannot understand their shape, their form, their color, and their dimension.

Above all these powers, we believe there is the most powerful and eternal power: namely, God. Though, as any other, we are incapable of seeing him, we are aware of his deeds to humans and the whole universe. While esteeming God as the Supreme Power, we believe in the light of the scriptures. He shared his power with humanity on two occasions. First, he shared his power with humans after creating the entire universe. He offered them the power of individuality. God gave us natural power to probe into the mysteries and unseen powers of nature. We have brought many of those natural powers under our control. This is why, with the Psalmist, we love to sing loudly: *"What is man that you are mindful of him; and a son of man that you care for him? Yet you have made him little less than a god, crowned him with glory and honor. You have given him rule over the works of your hands, put all things at his feet"* (Ps. 8:5–7).

And the second occasion when the Lord of the universe shared his power was the day of Pentecost, about which we meditate this weekend. He offered to the human beings the power of community—an energy to be together, a power to be united in diversities. The Bible tells us the disciples were together as one family, praying for the power. When they got it, we noticed their spirit of unity energized all the people of different races, of different languages, and of different cultures—they could hear everything the disciples spoke in their own tongues.

It is indeed hard for a natural man to be together with other people. Individually, we are gifted to dominate, to control, and to possess. But God wanted his human not to be a loner. An individual person cannot be full and whole unless he/she becomes a community person. This is why God poured down his power from on high to energize men and women to become a community. Traditionally, the church feels this is the day she was born. The church's main goal to be here on earth is to be a sign of that second creation, the second shower of God's power of community.

St. Paul beautifully states how the Holy Spirit becomes the center and core of making us live together. Without him, it's impossible for us to be together. However smart we may be, however diplomatic or politically correct we may behave, we will not arrive at a genuine unity or togetherness of humans without the power of the Holy Spirit. Paul affirms that no one can confess Jesus as Lord except in the Holy Spirit. This means, any effort to build up a community on the basis of confessing Jesus as the Lord cannot be possible; nor is it genuine if it does not start, continue, and end in his Spirit. He also tells us that all the gifts, charisms, ministries, and talents come from the same one Spirit, from one God, and for the one church. The individual manifestation or achievement is given for the sake of the common good, not for individual benefits.

Plus, the Apostle reminds us it is by and in the Spirit we are one body of Christ. Oneness comes by the presence of the Spirit. These days, it is very hard to bring people together. Not only the secular and the religious, not just different religious people, but much worse—those disciples who say they confess Jesus as their Lord, those who claim they have charisms from the Spirit, and those who are convinced they are the members of the true Body of Christ. We should be careful with those enemies inside the campus of the disciples of Jesus, who work against the Spirit of the community. We see many Christians behaving very individualistically and being injurious to the unity of the church. We can very easily identify those enemies of Christ. Any person who is always claiming his or her right and living an isolated life, or not interested in or hateful toward community life, is certainly a mini-Antichrist; he/

she is the agent of the devil who sneaked into the Garden of Eden and snatched away the first parents from God. We need both the power of individuality and the power of unity or community. The only possible solution for eradicating scandalous disunity among us is nothing but the empowerment of the Spirit.

TWENTY-SIXTH WEEKEND

Trinity Sunday
Our God Is Life, Love, and Communion

Therefore, since we have been justified by faith, we have peace with God through our Lord Jesus Christ, through whom we have gained access [by faith] to this grace in which we stand, and we boast in hope of the glory of God. Not only that, but we even boast of our afflictions, knowing that affliction produces endurance; and endurance, proven character; and proven character, hope; and hope does not disappoint, because the love of God has been poured out into our hearts through the Holy Spirit that has been given to us.

(Rom. 5:1–5)

One of the most controversial terms perennially debated in humanity is "God." It has become not only a contentious issue but also a source of fighting, terrorism, war, and murder around the globe. Due to so many versions and holdings and convictions about this name "God," millions of human beings are drifting away from that name—which a large portion of humanity esteems the same as the only life-giving force. From the beginning of the human race, people felt an inner and intrinsic connection between themselves and this God.

While they experienced him and his presence, they could not explain about him totally and fully. When their children asked them to explain about their God, they tried to offer some explanations; but these were always incomplete, such as "He is wisdom, power, force, nature, and even pleasure in itself." There are others who consider God as judge, destroyer, policeman, or a Sleeping Beauty. Many fell short of words that either most of them failed or were incomplete, or they even spoiled the integrity of God.

Therefore, many religions advise us to approach God as a "mystery" and behold his power and support through contemplation and meditation. Christianity, through its scriptures and tradition, has tried to describe this "mystery" as clearly as possible. So we believe God as Father, Son, and the Spirit—three in one. They, though different from each other, are united in equality. As St. Augustine would acknowledge, this description is still limited; though Jesus has delivered his revelation as complete and total, still, we—the humans—have to struggle to understand it. Hence in every age, solid attempts are made to know this mystery a little more clearly. In this postmodern age, possessing all kinds of research studies of different religions and their description of God and combining our own as Trinity, we can understand and meditate about our God in the following way, which is more relevant to our daily life.

Our God is the Father, meaning he is the Source of Life. The Hebrew term "Father, Abba" denotes the creativeness of God. He is the Source of all things in the universe. He maintains it; he protects it and destroys it. Everything is functioning according to his will. This is what Moses tells his people about their God, who was interacting with them as they made their journey to the Promised Land.

Our God is the Son, denoting he is the Source of Love. "God is love" is a theme of our religion and scriptures.

Jesus showed in his Incarnation by being the Son of God; he suffered and died for love of God and love of people. God becomes a victim of love, a sacrifice of love. He loved us first. He expects an intimacy of love in him and around him. In the second reading, Paul speaks about that intimacy of love that exists between God and Jesus and us.

And our God is the Holy Spirit, pointing out he is the Source of Communion: God is a communion floating in love. The Spirit Jesus introduced us to is the symbol of God's communion. He connected the Father with the Son Jesus, and he is connecting them with each and every one of us. This is what the Gospel of Jesus is all about. "Go to all nations and bring everyone to this communion. I shall be there among you until the end of ages." It is the Father and Jesus's Spirit of communion that remains forever with us. God is a family, a community, and a relationship.

This is what we believe in. This is what we participate in. We bring our children through baptism into this faith of God as our life, our love, and our communion. If you go to a psychologist and ask him to help you to find out who you are, he will answer you: "First, you tell me who your friend is, then I will tell you who you are." But if you come to a religious/spiritual counselor with the same question of who you are, he will surely reply: "First, you tell me what kind of God you profess to worship. I will surely tell you who you are."

It is a truthful fact of human behavior that its large portion is being influenced by each person's approach to the God figure. Let our lives then be attuned to God, whose identity we meditate on this weekend, and be shaped by it to the full.

TWENTY-SEVENTH WEEKEND

Corpus Christi Sunday
Eucharistic Transformation: Mysterious but Realistic

For I received from the Lord what I also handed on to you that the Lord Jesus, on the night he was handed over, took bread and, after he had given thanks, broke it and said, "This is my body that is for you. Do this in remembrance of me." In the same way also the cup, after supper, saying, "This cup is the new covenant in my blood. Do this, as often as you drink it, in remembrance of me." For as often as you eat this bread and drink the cup, you proclaim the death of the Lord until he comes. (1 Cor. 11:23–26)

This weekend, let us meditate on the remarkable ritual our Lord Jesus handed down to us through his disciples, as Paul puts it, before he left from this world. Through the Bible and church tradition we are exhorted, this ritual is the source for our spiritual experience. By participating in this ritual, we would get some incredible experiences—both internally and externally. It is called the "Eucharistic transformation," occurring in our life in three ways.

Firstly, we become persons of self-giving. The Sacrament of the Eucharist shows how Jesus gives himself, in total love, to be eaten by us. His self-giving was perfected and completed on the cross when he died, shedding the last drop of his blood for our salvation. Jesus, thus, gives himself totally for us. He gives until nothing is left to give. He loves his own as much as to sacrifice everything for his loved ones. Our participation in the Eucharist should make us less selfish and more self-giving, loving, caring, forgiving, and compassionate.

Secondly, our participation in this ritual energizes us to be life-giving: Jesus's self-giving was life-giving. Eucharist is true food and drink, which nourishes us and helps us share in the life of Jesus. *"Amen, amen, I say to you, unless you eat the flesh of the Son of Man and drink his blood, you do not have life within you"* (John 6:53). He communicates his life to his dear ones by sharing his own flesh and blood with them. He becomes one with us so that we may be transformed into his body. St. Augustine heard the words of the Lord in his prayer thus: "You will not change me into yourself as you would food of your flesh; but you will be changed into me." We become what we eat!

The life that the Eucharist gives is, of course, eternal life—as Jesus is the eternal Son of God. Our participation of the Eucharist challenges us to love, to promote, to uphold, and to defend life in all its forms, from the moment of conception to natural death. Just as the Lord shares himself in the life-giving sacrament, we need to share our own lives—our talents, time, and resources—with the needy.

The Eucharist also strengthens us to be unifying: Eucharist is the sacrament of unity. Jesus gave himself up for us to unify and reconcile humanity with God. Our participation in the Eucharist—which is a sacrament of forgiving love, unity, and reconciliation—should make us long for and work for reconciliation, peace, and harmony in our own families, communities, and the world at large.

By participating in the Eucharistic Mass, we would possess an amazing ability to see dualities—the pros and cons of situations as change approaches—and to quickly and efficiently think them through before making any decisions. We would dare to look deeply into our desires, regenerate self-awareness, and recognize psychological ambiguities. This will bring balance into our home and family life. We would pay attention to the details as we bring our inner and outer life into unity and harmony. Surely, we will enjoy the changes occurring within us! As we come to terms with ourselves, we would be able to see a more fulfilling purpose in life, and our field of experience broadens. We would focus on matters that affect us most deeply; and like magic, our life will become easier, and things will seem to take care of themselves. We will have all the necessary resources and motivation to make tangible changes and achieve results in all our endeavors. We will become unique persons who are self-giving, life-giving, and surely, unifying. In every step of our lives, we will develop into a peacemaker and peace lover. We will be energized to live like a true champion of Eucharistic unity at home, in the community, and around the nation.

Every time we participate in the Mass in communion with the body and blood of Jesus Christ, all those earlier-said results must be experienced by us. Today, Jesus invites us to rethink of our style of participation in the Eucharist—not only by meditating about it but also by making it our own possession and promising ourselves we will hold on to it in the days to come.

TWENTY-EIGHTH WEEKEND

Tenth Sunday of the Year
God Has Visited and Healed His People

Soon afterward, he journeyed to a city called Nain . . . As he drew near to the gate of the city, a man who had died was being carried out, the only son of his mother, and she was a widow . . . When the Lord saw her, he was moved with pity for her and said to her, "Do not weep." He stepped forward and touched the coffin; at this the bearers halted, and he said, "Young man, I tell you, arise!" The dead man sat up and began to speak, and Jesus gave him to his mother . . . (Luke 7:11–17)

Suffering and death are part and parcel of human life. The Spirit of God offers us some guidelines how to go about in these horrible but inevitable happenings of our life. This weekend, let us meditate about them.

When they happen in our own lives, God expects us to think of his life-giving goodness and compassion. We may hold various perspectives and views about them. One most prevalent among them is that God is angry with us because we have sinned against him; therefore, he punishes us or chastises us. It is a common assumption that suffering and sin were interconnected. Certainly, there are too many references of it in all the scriptures and in various religious traditions. Many times, we are tempted to retort to our religious mentors who visit us at our sickbed, saying like the widow of Zarephath: *"Why have you done this to me, O man of God? Have you come to me to call attention to my guilt and to kill my son?"* (1 Kings 17:18).

However, God thinks in a different way. We need to remember that in the Book of Job, in the Old Testament, God overturns the thinking of Job's friends, who had concluded that either he or his children might have sinned, which was why he was suffering. And so was Jesus when his disciples jumped to the conclusion that a man's blindness was the result of his sin (John 9:1–3). Rejecting the logic of his disciples, he said: *"Neither he nor his parents sinned; it is so that the works of God might be made visible through him."*

God is not just talking about the good results of our sufferings, in some way or another, through some of his messengers, does wonders in the lives of sufferers. As Old Testament prophets acted as healing and life-giving agents of God, we come to understand in the remarkable good deeds of Jesus performed in his earthly life. As we meditate this weekend on the Gospel passage, Jesus splendidly testifies the eternal truth that our God is not a God of death but of life and resurrection; our God is full of compassion and goodness. He never wants us to suffer or even die. Jesus was a staunch protector of life. He healed those whose lives were burdened by sickness and pain. He forgave sinners whose lives were sad and lonely because their sin alienated them from God and others. He reached out repeatedly to the poor, whose lives were broken by their need. While others avoided the dead so as not to risk ritual impurity, Jesus touched the dead and restored them to life. In the end, he would give his own life and submit to a torturous death in order to save sinners from death and assure them of life everlasting.

After we personally were strengthened and healed by our Master, we were advised by him to act as "wounded healers" and "resurrected persons" toward those who were burdened with such sufferings. We, the disciples of Jesus, are called to continue the prophetic ministry of caregiving and healing among our fellow men. Undoubtedly, it is a great burden that is thrust on each and every one of us. Actually, we do many things for the needy and the suffering and the dying—as spouses, as parents, as elders, as children, as doctors, as nurses, and as priests. Many times, this ministry doesn't offer any life and contentment to the beneficiaries as Jesus intends. This is because we always do this in a very natural and earthly way: out of emotions, feelings, pity, sympathy, or even out of some personal agenda behind it.

This caregiving service, according to God's Spirit, must not be merely a natural humanistic service to others in need. Every serviceable or caregiving action we perform must start with the goal of bringing out the glory of our God and not our own; we should continuously be connected closely with the risen Lord in prayer and discipline. We should conduct ourselves in this matter as Paul behaved: *"I want you to know, brothers and sisters, that the gospel preached by me is not of human origin. For I did not receive it from a human being, nor was I taught it, but it came through a revelation of Jesus Christ."*

Once we rise up and walk from the times of troubles and trials through our prayer and faith, our Master invites us to testify to it, shouting loud to our friends who are still in agony as the Psalmist sings: "The Lord brought me up from the netherworld; He preserved me from among those going to the pit; He changed my mourning into dancing. Yes, certainly He will do it to you also. Come, let us praise the Lord Most High!"

Eleventh Sunday of the Year
Everyone Is Entitled to a Second Chance

Now there was a sinful woman in the city who learned that he was at table in the house of the Pharisee . . . Then Jesus turned to the woman and said to Simon, "Do you see this woman? When I entered your house, you did not give me water for my feet, but she has bathed them with her tears and wiped them with her hair. You did not give me a kiss, but she has not ceased kissing my feet since the time I entered. You did not anoint my head with oil, but she anointed my feet with ointment. So I tell you, her many sins have been forgiven; hence, she has shown great love. But the one to whom little is forgiven, loves little." He said to her, "Your sins are forgiven." The others at table said to themselves, "Who is this who even forgives sins?" But he said to the woman, "Your faith has saved you; go in peace." Afterward he journeyed from one town and village to another, preaching and proclaiming the good news of the kingdom of God. Accompanying him were the twelve and some women who had been cured of evil spirits and infirmities—Mary, called Magdalene, from whom seven

> *demons had gone out; Joanna, the wife*
> *of Herod's steward Chuza; Susanna; and*
> *many others who provided for them out of*
> *their resources.* (Luke 7:36–8:3)

This weekend, the Spirit of God inspires us, offering a positive outlook about our fragile and weak life. Our God, being also just in his judgment, is very merciful and compassionate toward us, bestowing us a life-giving "second chance" whenever we fail him and ourselves in observing his laws. He has demonstrated this truth to mankind in his benevolent dealings with us. Throughout the scriptures, we observe this. When typical sinners like King David sinned, God—though he was infuriated in his justice—stoops down to him and offers pardon. When David cried out to God for forgiveness, the Lord immediately grants it to him (2 Sam. 12:7–13).

Jesus, the beloved Son of God, never ceased even a single moment to proclaim about the merciful character of our just God. In the Gospel passage we have taken this weekend for our meditation, Jesus attests himself to be the "friend of sinners," like his Father. When the natural-born blind humans were scandalized at his surprising move toward a public sinner in the presence of a very righteous and elite crowd, they questioned him for such impropriety. He paid no attention to them because he was busy in seeing in his heart his Father in heaven, with his angels rejoicing over this moment as the sinner demonstrated her atonement for her sins. She would travel farther down the road than any of those who were now judging her. By welcoming her and graciously accepting her, Jesus put wind in her sails. As a result of the sinful woman shedding tears of repentance at his feet, Jesus granted her a second chance to live a renewed life again; and she indeed began to live a new and better life.

Together with this woman, we notice that in Jesus's life, so many daredevil-women boldly approaching God in Jesus received forgiveness. The end result of this was their life was renewed, shaped, groomed, strengthened, and filled with joy and contentment. They had never experienced anything like this before. Jesus was the best person they had ever met. Hence they were not only forgiven, but loved by Jesus. By treating them with kindness, Jesus helped them to believe in their own power and goodness. They started following him wherever he went, always serving him in his needs.

In the same way, all Jesus's disciples have been experiencing this in their lives. Let us remember Paul as number 1 in this matter. He once had been the sinful and wretched Saul—but in the middle of his life, because of God's compassion, he got forgiveness with no precondition for it. This is why he loved to emphasize continuously in his Letters that all of us are justified not by our good deeds but by our faith in the mercy of God. Once we get forgiveness from God, we would join with Paul and dare enough to say: *"I have been crucified with Christ; yet I live, no longer I, but Christ lives in me; insofar as I now live in the flesh, I live by faith in the Son of God who has loved me and given himself up for me"* (Gal. 2:19–20).

There are many in our midst who won't accept the possibility that people can change. They are not willing to give people a second chance. A culture that doesn't believe in redemption is a culture without hope. Often, our guilt-feeling and fear prevent us from drawing close to the Lord. Let us humbly turn to the Lord with all our burden of sins, confident that we will find acceptance and forgiveness.

Also, with compassion and forgiveness, we have to relate ourselves to the persons whom we consider as sinners. Jesus, though he hates sin, does not condemn the sinners. Come, let us go to the forgiving table of the Lord and spread such merciful tables to all our sinful friends and relatives.

THIRTIETH WEEKEND

Twelfth Sunday of the Year
***"The Unrelenting Faith in Jesus,
the Doubly Anointed"***

*Once when Jesus was praying in solitude,
and the disciples were with him, he asked
them . . . "But who do you say that I
am?" Peter said in reply, "The Messiah of
God . . ." He said, "The Son of Man must
suffer greatly and be rejected by the
elders, the chief priests, and the scribes,
and be killed and on the third day be
raised." Then he said to all, "If anyone
wishes to come after me, he must deny
himself and take up his cross daily and
follow me. For whoever wishes to save his
life will lose it, but whoever loses his life
for my sake will save it."* (Luke 9:18–24)

We always admire the people who proclaim their
staunch faith in Jesus Christ that he is the "Messiah" as
Peter responded to Jesus's question, "Who do you say that
I am?" In the same vein, most of us continue to assure
ourselves and others, declaring the same profession of
faith. We love to insert in our prayers and hymns to Jesus
such wonderful faith-filled terms as the Psalmist uses in
his Psalm 63: *"O God, you are my God; you indeed are my
savior, and I will bless you as long as I live."*

Very surprisingly, in the Gospel passage of Luke, which
we meditate on this weekend, Jesus rebukes Peter for

such a profession. In narrating the same event, Matthew (16:13–23) and Mark (8:27–33), in their Gospels, offer us another version and background of the heartbreaking rebuke of Jesus against Peter. According to them, Jesus appreciates Peter for his profession of faith in him; but then he vehemently chides him, saying "'behind me, Satan'" when Peter rebukes Jesus, who foretells of his future suffering and death.

In the light of God's Word freely handed down to us in all the books of the Bible, we can draw a breathtaking lesson for our Christian life. The faith we uphold in Jesus as Christ the Messiah should be based on the understanding of the twofold messiahship of Jesus as anointed by God. In the culture of Judaism, we read there were so many leaders anointed with the oil either of kingship or of priesthood. Only Jesus was both king and priest; because he had come to fulfill the law, he alone possessed the twofold perfection of kingship and priesthood.

Our Savior, however, who is the Christ, a unique Messiah, has been anointed by the Holy Spirit as he himself claimed: *"The Spirit of the Lord is upon me because he has anointed me."* He declared and foretold throughout his life the godly anointing he got from his Father was not only of power and glory, but also of sufferings and death, only through which he would covet God's glory. That is what we hear him sharing with his disciples in the Gospel. *"The Son of Man must suffer greatly and be rejected by the elders, the chief priests, and the scribes, and be killed and on the third day be raised."*

All Old Testament prophets like Zechariah prophesied so about Jesus: *". . . when they look on him whom they have thrust through, they will mourn for him as one mourns for an only child, and they will grieve for him as one grieves over a firstborn*" (Zech. 12:10b). The prophetic words summed up the twofold identity of Jesus—namely, he had to go through rejections, condemnations, and horrible sufferings from humankind, who would, at the end, salute him and honor him as their leader. When Jesus asked the question "Who do you say that I am?" he wanted Peter to say "You are the kingly but suffering servant Messiah." It is for such identity Jesus came to this world, took the form of a slave, and underwent ignominious death: death on the cross. He came, he suffered, and he died so that people like Peter could know his immense love for them and appreciate his unbearable sufferings—his bleeding and death for the sake of their salvation.

In this way, Jesus expects us today to identify him as the Suffering Servant Messiah. Most people in the world today acknowledge Jesus as the founder of the largest religion, a revolutionary Jewish reformer, a great teacher, and a man of peace. His teachings have transformed the lives of an incredible number of people. He can indeed be termed as the single most influential person who ever lived in world history. No other person in history has occupied so much space in books, poetry, paintings, and sculptures. Yet all these do not make him what he truly is: the Savior of the world and our personal Savior. But we, the disciples of Jesus, do.

Let us purify our faith in Jesus—not only esteem his messiahship as the source of glory and power but also truthfully embrace his boldness and stamina to bear the consequences of following his footsteps of justice and love, namely, unprecedented sufferings and even ignominious death. Is he our Savior, the Lord and master of our life? What influence does he have in our life's plans, programs, choices, priorities, and decisions? If we begin to live in his way, at times, it may bring to us unbearable sufferings and hardships. Christ demands that we have to bear them as the cross with him. Are we ready? But don't you worry: he is our "com-pan-ion" in life. Literally—the one who breaks bread with us. We will win the War.

THIRTY-FIRST WEEKEND

Thirteenth Sunday of the Year
Christ Set Us Free from the Yoke of Slavery

When the days for his being taken up were fulfilled, he resolutely determined to journey to Jerusalem, and he sent messengers ahead of him. On the way, they entered a Samaritan village to prepare for his reception there, but they would not welcome him because the destination of his journey was Jerusalem. When the disciples James and John saw this, they asked, "Lord, do you want us to call down fire from heaven to consume them?" Jesus turned and rebuked them, and they journeyed to another village. The would-be followers of Jesus. As they were proceeding on their journey, someone said to him, "I will follow you wherever you go." Jesus answered him, "Foxes have dens and birds of the sky have nests, but the Son of Man has nowhere to rest his head . . ."

(Luke 9:51–62)

We know well how almost all of us, with our good and splendid brains, use certain goals and targets in the process of achieving success. They may be small as short-term goals, or sometimes long-term goals that take so much of our time and energy and our sweat and blood. It is our experience that such successes seem to be very temporary and short-lived. In the light of Jesus, our Master, we know that in order to lead a self-fulfilling and soul-enriching life of happiness till our last breath that is extended even after our death, we indeed need a long-term goal. Jesus called it eternal life.

This eternal life, according to Jesus, is an uninterrupted life of bliss, a life of true freedom, a life of peace, and a life of full contentment. To attain this life-term goal, the Gospel passage we have taken for this weekend meditation offers us some practical and radical ways. These ways can be summed up under two categories: attachment to the goal and detachment from anything that obstructs, deviates, and distracts us from achieving our goal.

Any goal-achieving effort demands we have to discover our goal, fix it to our mind and heart. Once we find out eternal life as our goal, then we need to put our hearts into it. Luke underscores it in a metaphorical way, how Jesus was heading toward the final destiny of Jerusalem. This means Jesus determinately journeyed to Jerusalem to undergo whatever was necessary for his work to be completed. In this resolute journey of life, he followed the footsteps of his forebears like Prophet Elisha, who— to signal his commitment to the prophetic ministry of Elijah—left all his properties and his likings, which he demonstrated by burning his plow and roasting his oxen to feed his people. Elisha vividly proved his conviction that he would be no longer leaning on his fields and flocks to secure his future as any well-to-do farmer did; but once he had accepted to walk the walk of Elijah, he would be completely dependent on God from then onward (1 Kings 19:16–21).

Jesus did live that way from the onset of his journey to the earth. He emptied himself and left all his glory and blissful life with his Father and angels in heaven; he took the form of a slave, literally meaning that he had very little worldly possessions. He did not even have a place of his own to rest and depended largely on God and his people. Jesus commands those who desire to follow him to do the same. Almost all his disciples, starting from those twelve till this day, leave everything behind once and for all and follow the Master.

We know why Jesus sets before us some such hard ways to be followed. We carry lots of monkeys on our back, willingly or unwillingly, to survive in this earthly life. They are a nuisance many a time, as a kind of large yoke to be borne. Many times, we feel we need them. But Jesus wants us to get rid of those monkeys totally and completely and follow him. Thus, he expects his disciples to be solely dependent on God and his providence.

When we start following Jesus resolutely the way he sketched out, sometimes we may seem hardheaded or freaky; we should give in to such criticism. However, we shouldn't behave like those brothers James and John in the Gospel either, to be short-tempered and quick-fixing. Never get overwhelmed by your own puny wisdom and perfection-model; rather, converse with Jesus, our life-companion. Let us not lose heart but get going in the path of Jesus, fixing our minds and hearts to the final goal: eternal life. Consequently, even in this world, our lives would be permeated with the true freedom and joy that Jesus promised. Then for the rest of our lives till death, we will hilariously proclaim with Paul: *"For freedom, Christ set me free; so I stand firm, and I do not submit again to the yoke of slavery"* (Gal. 5:1).

THIRTY-SECOND WEEKEND

Fourteenth Sunday of the Year
We're the Witnesses of God's Abundance

After this, the Lord appointed seventy-two others, whom he sent ahead of him in pairs to every town and place he intended to visit. He said to them, "The harvest is abundant, but the laborers are few; so ask the master of the harvest to send out laborers for his harvest. Go on your way; behold, I am sending you like lambs among wolves. Carry no money bag, no sack, no sandals . . . Whoever listens to you, listens to me. Whoever rejects you, rejects me. And whoever rejects me, rejects the one who sent me . . . Behold, I have given you the power 'to tread upon serpents and scorpions' and upon the full force of the enemy, and nothing will harm you. Nevertheless, do not rejoice because the spirits are subject to you, but rejoice because your names are written in heaven." (Luke 10:1–20)

Through the revelation of God in Jesus, we are made to understand that our God is the God of abundance, an unlimited stock of all goodness. We can observe this fact in all his abundant creations. He too is plentiful in his redemptive works. We notice in his every movement and interaction with human beings all his richness, especially his mercy, love, compassion, wisdom, and power. He deliberately desired to make us understand and enjoy such remarkable abundance. Through Prophet Isaiah, he proudly invites us humans to enjoy in him all his blessings and gifts as from a rejoicing and loving mother (Isa. 66:10–14).

To enlighten us in this regard, he sent his beloved Son, Jesus, to us as an eyewitness and spokesperson. Jesus faithfully obeyed his Father and lived up to his expectation. However, as a human being, Jesus's life was short and very limited. He witnessed to his Father's abundance through his preaching and healing in and around Palestine as much as he could and as long as he could. As the Gospels verify, there were many places Jesus intended to go—but he could not, to fulfill his ministry. Hence, he appointed many apostles and disciples, not to replace him but rather to represent him and his ministry to those people whom he could not reach. He too underscored there are already plentiful blessings ready to be harvested. He longed many of his humans cooperate with him in harvesting them.

He wanted his disciples to go and bear witness to his cause and bring many human persons into his fellowship. He categorically told them the only weapon, ammunition, or resource they can carry with them for their power and strength was sole dependence on their God of abundance and not money, politics, diplomacy, or human intelligence. Rather, the unimaginable power to win over or persuade humans successfully in their ministry entirely depends on one single principle or strategy—namely, total dependence on his God of abundance. This is why he asked them not to take with them anything more than the basic necessities.

For more than two millennia, Jesus continues his ministry of witnessing to his Father's abundance of love, compassion, wisdom, and power through his selected apostles. We who are meditating this weekend on this historical truth belong to that group of chosen ones to continue Jesus's ministry. He has appointed us and sent us to our individual life situations to continue his witnessing ministry. From his abundance, he has endowed us with limitless faith, hope, and charity. Above all, he has graced us with an attitude of dependence on the God of abundance. We are bearing on us, as Paul writes, the marks of Jesus, the Crucified (Gal. 6:14–18). This means all his disciples are marked with the mind-setup of Jesus to depend only on God for all our abundance.

We know what we are and how much material and intellectual resources we possess. But we are rich and abundant in our faith, hope, and charity. Thus, we testify to a God who has chosen the weak like us to defeat the strong. While two-thirds of Christians in this world behave smartly in being indifferent to church-witnessing and feel they are wise enough to withdraw their involvement in God's ministries, the other one-third are selected and chosen by Jesus to show the world how our God of abundance has recreated our personal, family, and community life inside his church of abundance. So many development projects in this world have been accomplished over the centuries—not by those who esteem themselves being too smart to enjoy individual independence and self-gratification and being fattened by possessions of riches and properties, but by spiritual abundance of widows and widowers, the old and weak, and the poor and the sick who are indeed the small group of Jesus's committed disciples.

This makes us rejoice with the Psalmist (Ps. 66), singing praises to the glory of God today and every day. Not that we have fully accomplished in life what was designed by God in Jesus; rather, that we are included in his team of witnesses at present. Many times, it may seem as a thankless task to continue Jesus's ministry in this world of darkness and blindness; however, let us be assured by the promises of Jesus who says: *"Nevertheless, don't rejoice because the evil spirits submit to you; rejoice rather that your names are written in heaven."*

THIRTY-THIRD WEEKEND

Fifteenth Sunday of the Year
Help the Needy on Their "Bloody Path" to Heaven

Jesus replied, "A man fell victim to robbers as he went down from Jerusalem to Jericho. They stripped and beat him and went off leaving him half-dead. A priest happened to be going down that road, but when he saw him, he passed by on the opposite side. Likewise, a Levite came to the place, and when he saw him, he passed by on the opposite side. But a Samaritan traveler who came upon him was moved with compassion at the sight. He approached the victim, poured oil and wine over his wounds, and bandaged them. Then he lifted him up on his own animal, took him to an inn, and cared for him. The next day, he took out two silver coins and gave them to the innkeeper with the instruction, 'Take care of him. If you spend more than what I have given you, I shall repay you on my way back.' Which of these three, in your opinion, was neighbor to the robbers' victim?" He answered, "The one who treated him with mercy." Jesus said to him, "Go and do likewise."

(Luke 10:30–37)

The lovers of the love-command of Jesus get the name "Good Samaritans" from the parable of Jesus, which we meditate on this weekend. The Samaritan in the story was there to help the man at the time and place of his need. The word *neighbor* in the dictionary of Jesus means "one who is in need" and not "one who is in proximity" or "one who is close to us." Among the three in the parable who happen to meet the person suffering and bleeding on the roadside, one was a Samaritan who seemed to be a good one, upholding love and mercy as the only norms for his life. There were no strings attached up or behind his life schedule as those other two so-called holy people, the temple priest and the Levite. There was no prejudice on which he based his relationships or help. He had no busy schedule of accomplishments or enterprises that distracted or diverted him from doing this love deed. He had no better or bigger priorities than volunteering to help the needy. He helped the needy in whatever way he could and afford to do. He too went out of his way to carry the man to the inn, where he paid his board and lodging.

We know well Jesus was a typical Good Samaritan. He has proved it and witnessed to it at many times. He is quoted saying at his farewell discussion, "Love your neighbors as I have loved you." He too had declared that as a good friend and good shepherd, he laid down his life for his neighbors. All this spirit of love—combined with justice, service, and sacrifice—was inherited by him from his Heavenly Father. His Father is a God of love. Jesus professed and wanted us also to believe that *"God so loved the world that He sent his only begotten Son, so that everyone who believes in him might not perish but might have eternal life"* (John 3:16). God's eternal love has no partiality. That is God's love of perfection.

Following his Heavenly Father, Jesus lived a perfect life of love as a Good Samaritan. He started his life in love of his Father, and he continued it with the same love till the end. Surprisingly, he demonstrated that "love" through his neighborly love. He knew his Father gave to humanity one and only command for their prosperous and fuller life: namely, "*love God with your whole heart and your whole being.*" At the same time, Jesus too believed, unhesitantly, what his Father declared through Moses about observing his love-command. *"For this command which I am giving you today is not too wondrous or remote for you. It is not in the heavens . . . No, it is something very near to you, in your mouth and in your heart, to do it"* (Deut. 30:9–14). In other words, Jesus understood that his Father expected his humans to demonstrate their love for him by loving their neighbors, who are around them.

This is why Jesus was found anywhere and anytime the humans were in need. He taught love to the crowd. He took his cross, hung on it, and died by it. He candidly and repeatedly stated the requirement to attain eternal life is to love our neighbors, and he emphasized it by the parable of the Good Samaritan. He too is quoted saying, about the final judgment, that he would judge us according to our love deeds and not according to any other religious or even spiritual deeds. Good Samaritans' love deeds are the ladders that take us to heaven.

The evil force is roaring like a lion to devour us and tries to make our life dangerous and risky. Jesus used relevantly in his parable a road that ran between Jerusalem to Jericho, which was called Bloody Pass. It was a dangerous road where journey was so risky, so dangerous, and so unsafe. Human life too is a precarious path to heaven. In order to make life safe, to free and heal people from their wounds and dangers, Jesus longs for all his disciples to act like him. He expects us to act as his hands, his feet, his heart, and his body. He demands that we should get down from our donkeys (as the Samaritan of the parable did) of indifference, complacence, pride, coldness, and ignorance. All for nothing but to prove that we love our Father in heaven wholeheartedly.

Sixteenth Sunday of the Year
Let's Do the Works of the Lord,
Knowing the Lord of the Works

As they continued their journey, he entered a village where a woman, whose name was Martha, welcomed him. She had a sister named Mary [who] sat beside the Lord at his feet, listening to him speak. Martha, burdened with much serving, came to him and said, "Lord, do you not care that my sister has left me by myself to do the serving? Tell her to help me." The Lord said to her in reply, "Martha, Martha, you are anxious and worried about many things. There is need of only one thing. Mary has chosen the better part, and it will not be taken from her."

(Luke 10:38–42)

The Gospel verses chosen for this weekend meditation narrate the story of two sisters, Martha and Mary. While the former is shown busy with the work of the Lord, the latter is more interested in knowing the Lord of the work. For Martha, doing service to Jesus seems first; but for Mary, it is holding a relationship with him. Traditionally, that is how this story has been interpreted. The bleak part of this interpretation is, quoting Jesus, *"Mary has chosen the better part,"* to let us esteem erroneously that any person choosing religious or ascetical vocation is holier and better than those that have taken up with the activities of everyday life in the world. This sort of thinking came out of dejecting the Gospel value proclaimed on this occasion and meaning that a quiet life of contemplation and prayer, personified in Mary, is superior to a busy life of activity and action, personified in Martha.

Jesus indeed loved to visit Bethany, home of these two sisters who were considered by him the best hosts with TLC (tender, loving care). They followed their Jewish tradition of hospitality from the time of Abraham and Sarah, who believed every guest coming to their home was a God-sent proxy (Gen. 18:1–10). In the person of Jesus, they recognized an extraordinary messenger of God. Both of them pleased the Lord, and that was why he chose them as signs to witness one of his most promising value of the Kingdom. He therefore did not intend to disparage Martha and her activity—but rather to show that hearing the Word of God is the foundation of all action, that the Word of God must permeate all other concerns.

For example, it is right that parents be entirely concerned and completely involved in the activity of raising their children—but first and always in the light of the Word of God. That is, all our secular activity must flow from or be based upon or be an expression of the Word of God. Therefore, to hear the Word of God is the absolute prerequisite for right action, the daily action of doing what Jesus said is the one thing necessary—namely, the building up of the Kingdom of God in the world. In other words, prayer is not better than action in the sense that they are contrary or contradictory realities, one to be chosen over the other; but rather, prayer is primary in the sense of being like the source of a stream, while action is like being the flow of that same stream. They are continuous and complementary and mutually dependent. Prayer without action is sterile, and action without prayer is empty. Ultimately, scripture is not calling us to one as better than the other, but rather, to embrace both. Only one who has become the hearer of the Word can truly become a doer of the Word.

Jesus liked his disciples to respect the inner and intrinsic connection between closely attaching to God's Word and intensely serving his people. Paul has been the most praiseworthy role model in this regard. Writing to the Colossians, he testifies his seamless striving to uphold this connection: *"Now I rejoice in my sufferings for your sake, and in my flesh I am filling up what is lacking in the afflictions of Christ on behalf of his body, which is the church . . . It is he whom we proclaim, admonishing everyone and teaching everyone with all wisdom, that we may present everyone perfect in Christ"* (Col. 1:24–28).

And so with all our saints. St. Teresa of Lisieux, a contemplative nun, wrote: *"To give the Lord a perfect hospitality, it is necessary that Mary and Martha must be joined as one."*

THIRTY-FIFTH WEEKEND

Seventeenth Sunday of the Year
Be a Daring Child to Enter into God's Chamber

> *I tell you, ask and you will receive; seek and you will find; knock and the door will be opened to you. For everyone who asks, receives; and the one who seeks, finds; and to the one who knocks, the door will be opened. What father among you would hand his son a snake when he asks for a fish? Or hand him a scorpion when he asks for an egg? If you then, who are wicked, know how to give good gifts to your children, how much more will the Father in heaven give the Holy Spirit to those who ask him?"* (Luke 11:9–13)

Every religion is nothing but a pool of ways and means, values and convictions, to unite humans with God. As Christians, we believe that God created humans in his likeness; and in the Garden of Eden, our first parents were walking with God and talking with him face-to-face. We also know that because of the sins of humanity, most of them failed to be on the road with God. They were dissipated. Some took the wrong route; others stopped their journey in between for their own gratification. Many were even rejected by God because of their injustice and infidelity.

However, a few strived to be loyal to God. They followed his directions, did their homework promptly, and tried to walk with God till their death. Abraham was one such faithful person who was persevering in his deals with God, and we read in the Bible how both conversed with each other with so much intimacy and confidence. There was wonderful relationship between them; there was a give-and-take policy and a friendly but justice-based negotiation going on in their conversation (Gen. 18:20–32). This is nothing but pure interpersonal communication between two persons in which we find emotions, rationality, and intimacy meet together; both parties enjoy a spiritual intercourse. The same amazing experience is also found in the lives of Jacob, Moses, Joshua, and many other patriarchs, judges, prophets, kings, and queens.

When Jesus lived in this world, he never missed even a single moment in communing with God. He esteemed God as his beloved Father, and superbly, his conviction was affirmed directly from God many times in private prayer time. But it was publicly affirmed a few times with a loud voice: "You are my beloved Son in whom I am well-pleased." This spiritual communing with his Father put him at rest and gave him sanity in the midst of sufferings, oppositions, and failures. Except sin, he experienced every bit of life's challenges as all of us. He too knew what human frailty was and how each one of his followers would be tossed by life-threatening tsunamis of perils and afflictions. Hence, he offered us an action plan of prayer. As he tasted and experienced this marvelous communing in prayer, he desired his disciples should also benefit from such encounters.

Jesus not only showed how we can relate ourselves with God in prayer, but also as Paul exclaims in his letter: *"He brought us to life along with him, having forgiven us all our transgressions, obliterating the bond against us, with its legal claims, which was opposed to us, he also removed it from our midst, nailing it to the cross"* (Col. 2:13–14). By his bleeding death, he brought reconciliation between God and humans; and he succeeded in making us the adopted children of God and bestowed to us an amazing ability to call him "Abba, Father."

He also taught us how to pray a quality prayer, which can be performed in spirit and in truth, in trust and in hope, and which would be spiritually beneficial. That is the message Jesus offers us this weekend (Luke 11:1–13). He wants us to follow him in using our prayer tool. We should relate ourselves to God—not with fear or any strangeness but more with being intimate, close, and personal. He asks us to demand our Father, persist in asking, persevere in petitioning, show confidence and dependency like a child, and never lose heart. Don't leave him without his saying "Okay, my child. Let it happen to you as you desire."

This means prayer is not to be taken as a mere bundle of prayers to be recited; nor as ordo of some religious ceremonies to be enacted. Rather, it is a constant and intimate communion with God. We should never think of God as a white-bearded Santa delivering blessings and gifts at our appeals; nor should we make him appear as a judge and face him at his court. Rather, we should dare to go into his private chamber. We must remember always Jesus's words: we deal with a person in prayer and not with a power, an energy, an idol, or a sleeping beauty.

THIRTY-SIXTH WEEKEND

Eighteenth Sunday of the Year
"Our Life's Road to Babylon or Jerusalem?"

There was a rich man whose land produced a bountiful harvest. He asked himself, "What shall I do, for I do not have space to store my harvest?" And he said, "This is what I shall do: I shall tear down my barns and build larger ones. There I shall store all my grain and other goods, and I shall say to myself, 'Now as for you, you have so many good things stored up for many years, rest, eat, drink, be merry!'" But God said to him, "You fool, this night your life will be demanded of you; and the things you have prepared, to whom will they belong?" Thus will it be for the one who stores up treasure for himself but is not rich in what matters to God."

(Luke 12:16–21)

Those of us who possess an active and sharp brain are troubled by the negative and dark side of humanity. In particular, the thought that we are nothing but dust, and that we will one day become dust unto dust, kills our peace and balance in active life. It is true many among us undergo same kind of feelings whenever we come across the scriptural words we have taken this weekend for our meditation. Some may mistakenly think that all religions promote, through their scriptures, only these negative values against life on earth. These are partly right and partly wrong.

Undoubtedly, in the Bible, we come across so many references on the dark and evil side of human life. For example, we read in the Book of Ecclesiastes: *"Vanity of vanities, all things are vanity . . . For what profit comes to mortals from all the toil and anxiety of heart with which they toil under the sun?"* (Eccl. 1:2; 2:21–23). And David sings about humans: *"Before a watch passes in the night, you wash them away . . ."* (Ps. 90:5–6). Such verses are pervasively spread in the scriptures. People who don't deeply enter into the Spirit behind these words would certainly be depressed and hostile. These words are truly like bitter capsules to be swallowed but for our sane living. We have to humbly and openly recognize our fragile and weak condition as creatures. Even though we are capable of inventions, creativeness, scientific discoveries, and so on— we are, after all, human creatures, pots made by someone supremely greater than us, the Creator God. Rational beings as we are may find it hard, humbling ourselves and accepting this bitter truth.

Nonetheless, it is inevitable; all that we hold as our material possessions will one day be gone from us, or we from them. Moreover, we know that money can buy us a good bed, but not a peaceful sleep. It will provide us with the best of cosmetics, but not the inner beauty of a loving heart. It can fill our life with amusements and pleasures, but it can never lead us to that inner peace and joy. As Jesus said, our life does not consist of possessions.

This does not mean God desires us to be lazy, to be broke, to be paupers and living on others' pockets. He commanded us to work and labor and earn our livelihood. He willed that we should be blessed with his riches, with his talents, with his energy and power. He wanted us to enjoy the rich harvest and fruits of the earth. He wanted us to be fertile, to enlarge our territories. He too blessed all his sons and daughters who were close to him with abundance of possessions. However, God always blessed only those who were entirely dependent on his sovereignty and power. He ignored those who forgot him while they were in pursuit of material possessions. Nor was he near to them who forgot him and his justice when they were filled with abundance, as the "rich fool" in Jesus's parable.

Christian life is a journey, not a home. The end of our journey is not death; death is only a golden key that opens the palace of eternity where God reigns. Material things are very useful in our lives, and so we are called not to become greedy and cling to our riches. By giving and giving of ourselves, we make treasures in heaven and become rich in the sight of God. Paul emphasizes this age-old human strategy, writing: *"Seek what is above, where Christ is seated at the right hand of God. Think of what is above, not of what is on earth. When Christ your life appears, then you too will appear with him in glory."*

Indeed, for our survival in this world, we have to make money and appropriate power, popularity, and a good name. Jesus knew about this fact. However, he warned us not to make those needed things as our idols. According to God's Word, it's hard for such idol worshippers to enter into the home sweet home. There are two roads for our life's journey. Both are in parallel, but each go opposite. One goes to the Babylon of tribulation, and the other to a Jerusalem of bliss. People love to choose to drive on the road to Babylon, during which they have hectic days and sleepless nights. If they have to take the Jerusalem road, there is a U-turn facility. Many have taken it and changed their life's direction, even at their deathbed.

As we have to take care of our survival and development in earthly life, we too must care for our spiritual life. We are born for greater things. Our home is not here. We are only on our journey to our Father's House. Let us dwell on these things this weekend and till the end of our earthly life.

Nineteenth Sunday of the Year
The Holy Ones Share Alike the
Same Blessings and Dangers

Gird your loins and light your lamps and be like servants who await their master's return from a wedding, ready to open immediately when he comes and knocks. Blessed are those servants whom the master finds vigilant on his arrival. Amen, I say to you, he will gird himself, have them recline at table, and proceed to wait on them. And should he come in the second or third watch and find them prepared in this way, blessed are those servants. Be sure of this: if the master of the house had known the hour when the thief was coming, he would not have let his house be broken into. You also must be prepared, for at an hour you do not expect, the Son of Man will come. (Luke 12:35–40)

Our life is made of both day and night, joy and sorrow, blessings and curses, uphills and downhills. Every human experiences it, and willy-nilly, they have to go through this paradoxical life path. Whenever we come across verses like "night" and "day" in the scriptures—most of the time, they mean the darkness-filled and light-encircled situations we meet in day-to-day life. When Jesus was talking about the vigilance of his disciples waiting for their Master, he pointed out that they should be ready—as Mark explains—in the evening, at midnight, or in the early morning. While most of the New Testament writers refer this night vigil to the waiting for the Parousia of the Lord, they never deny these night-experiences are the metaphors signifying the disasters, calamities, dangers, and tribulations humans undergo. Luke very well spells out this sort of waiting is not merely for the end-time arrival but much more for being faithful to Jesus's instructions in the period of Parousia.

In these life situations of difficulties and perils, God in Jesus invites us not to be agitated but to strive to be cool and maintain our mental and emotional balance as our holy ancestors, even in their dark days, were celebrating the Lord's name and their life with him. *"For in secret the holy children of the good were offering sacrifice and carried out with one mind the divine institution, so that your holy ones should share alike the same blessings and dangers"* (Wis. 18:6–9). To encounter both blessings and dangers in our life with smiling faces, God instructs us this weekend through his scriptural passages about an effective tool, which is called faith.

Faith is considered by our church tradition as one of the theological virtues. The Book of Wisdom tells us that faith is simply a human ascent of intellect and will. *"That night was known beforehand to our Fathers; with sure knowledge of the oaths in which they put their faith"* (Wis. 18:6). And in the Letter to the Hebrews, we read: *"Faith is confident assurance concerning what we hope for, and conviction about things we do not see"* (Heb. 11:1). Faith, therefore, is a reality of human capacity to dream dreams. It is an ascent of human intellect and will about a reality that is not there at present, which is unseen and unheard—a virtual reality. It's simply a human thing.

Faith also is a virtue of perseverance in pursuing certain things that are not available at present. It is "chutzpah," the human spirit of impudence, certain nerve or guts to put out into deep water, to launch some daredevil activities without any tangible hold. As the Lord Jesus indicates in the Gospel, faith is the spirit of a faithful and farsighted steward, waiting and waiting for great things to happen. *"Let your belts be fastened around your waists and your lamps be burning ready. Be like humans awaiting their master's return from a wedding"* (Luke 12:35).

Faith also is a virtue maintained and grown by human efforts. Simply storing certain truths and values in our intellect, even showering certain emotional kudos or appreciation toward them, will not nurture faith. Rather, with the seed of faith the humans have to work on. Interpreting our Lord's words about our vigilant services even at the time of darkness, the biblical scholars underline that "the vigilant waiting that is emphasized in the Gospel is a faithful accomplishment of duties at hand, with awareness that the end, for which the disciples must always be ready, will entail the great judgment by which the everlasting destiny of all will be determined."

Once our faith is matured and stronger, then it does a marvelous job in our lives. Faith is a powerful instrument to handle the unfairness of life successfully. According to the study done some years back by the Gallup Institute's religious research center in New Jersey, approximately 13 percent of believers were found to be most religiously committed. They are fully engaged in doing something with their faith seed, very faithful in their religious practices. The empirical evidences show that the benefits of faith in those people's lives are numerous. Their vibrant faith has transformed them into more ethical and honest people; more tolerant, respectful, and accepting of persons of different ethnicities or race and social, political, or economic backgrounds; more apt to perform acts of kindness, offer charitable services, volunteer services, and so on; and far happier than those with little, weak, or no faith to sustain them. Where do we stand now regarding our faith?

Twentieth Sunday of the Year
True Peace Only by Blazing Fire

I have come to set the earth on fire, and how I wish it were already blazing! There is a baptism with which I must be baptized, and how great is my anguish until it is accomplished! Do you think that I have come to establish peace on the earth? No, I tell you, but rather division. From now on a household of five will be divided, three against two and two against three; a father will be divided against his son and a son against his father, a mother against her daughter and a daughter against her mother, a mother-in-law against her daughter-in-law and a daughter-in-law against her mother-in-law. (Luke 12:49–53)

In this weekend, we hear from Jesus some alarming statements among which one is very provoking: *"I have come not to bring peace but division."* The critics of practicing religion would cynically agree with it because it is a common opinion that religions are the major source of division, suffering, and war disturbing our world. This statement of the Master also would shock all his disciples of peace. Very surprisingly, it sounds contradictory of the whole message of the Gospel. At the Last Supper, Jesus told his disciples: *"Peace I leave with you; my peace I give to you; not as the world gives do I give it to you. Do not let your hearts be troubled or afraid"* (John 14:27). Matthew quotes Jesus declaring in his Sermon on the Mount: *"Blessed are the peacemakers, for they shall be called the children of God."* Can we believe such a Prince of Peace could utter such controversial words? We need to give pause before our judgment and try to go deeper into his statement, by which he might have meant something other than what we understand at its surface level. In the light of the Spirit and of the works of church fathers and biblical scholars, we discover that Jesus didn't say anything negative about peace—but rather, positively, he has been concerned about the "true peace."

We should know no human being can survive even a single moment without some sort of inner peace. Physically, emotionally, and mentally—a person should be in balance. Every bit of our human system within us must be at its balanced level. This is called tranquility. If that normal level is lost, problems start in the body, mind, and soul. However, this tranquility can be disturbed or distorted by many of our unwanted activities. No human person can say he/she passes through daily life with no disturbance whatsoever. Thus, our peace is gone. During that critical situation, we are used to make recourse to many strategies to bring back that mental and emotional balance.

We think we can bring back our peace by perverted and undue physical pleasures like alcohol, drugs, perverted sex, even unlimited food and parties; by disturbing other people's peace by fighting against them and by including them in our company of miserable, low-spirited people; by being busy in our pursuit of money, becoming workaholics, turning out to be too extreme in our worldviews; by becoming champions of community causes and by making use of religion and devotion as a cover-up mechanism in order to avoid any trouble at home or in the office; by trying to bring peace in other people's lives or other neighborhoods, even other nations, by waging wars . . . war for war and violence for violence; and above all, by our compromises and complacency.

Sure, we will establish peace by such endeavors, but that peace is always temporary and fake. But Jesus came to proclaim about true peace, not as the world and earthly gimmicks offer. He also gave us some effective tools to achieve this true peace. This is what we hear him state in our weekend Gospel. He exhorts us to be burned with his fire of truth, justice, and love. *"I have come to set the earth on fire, and how I wish it were already blazing!"* Once this fire is burning within us, surely there will be lots of things and even persons, our near and dear ones have to be knocked out. Division starts there between the spirit of committed disciples and the spirit of complacent and indifferent people. He wants us to meet such chances as challenges of faith in him and stand in the battle and never to quit.

In this struggle, the Word of God encourages us, pointing out that millions of witnesses who have gone that way are with us. They put their lives on the line in defense of a way of life that they passionately believed in and fought for truth, justice, human rights, and the basic freedom that is everyone's sacred right. God wants us to join the club. In the lives of prophets like Jeremiah, we observe the kind of conflict we would face when we are loyal to our discipleship. When Jeremiah tells the people in plain words what is really happening and why it is occurring exactly as God inspires him to preach, people do not want to hear it. They refuse to listen and attack the prophet. But the prophet stood his ground of faith and found true peace within him (Jer. 38:4–6, 8–10). As the author of the Letter to the Hebrews cheers us, we are indeed surrounded by a cloud of witnesses to Jesus's fire blazing and dispelling darkness in the world, enlightening every one of God's children. Let us take such a fire of justice, truth, and love in our hands. Let us run the race of life while keeping our eyes fixed on Jesus, who has already won the race.

THIRTY-NINTH WEEKEND

Twenty-First Sunday of the Year
Narrow Gate to Wide Chamber of Bliss

> *Someone asked Jesus, "Lord, will only a few people be saved?" He answered them, "Strive to enter through the narrow door, for many, I tell you, will attempt to enter but will not be strong enough. After the master of the house has arisen and locked the door, then will you stand outside knocking and saying, 'Lord, open the door for us.' He will say to you in reply, 'I do not know where you are from . . . you yourselves will be cast out. And people will come from the east and the west and from the north and the south and will recline at table in the kingdom of God. For behold, some are last who will be first, and some are first who will be last.'"* (Luke 13:22–30)

Someone asked Jesus in the Gospel, "Will only a few people be saved?" Jesus's reply to this question is one of his hard sayings: *"Only those who go through the narrow gate will be saved."* What does he mean by "narrow gate"? The narrow gate, according to Jesus, is nothing but a human earthly life led in discipline. It is a life that is groomed, shaped, tamed, molded, and disciplined by the spirit of his Beatitudes of the Sermon on the Mount. If we reflect over those beatitudes in the light of what Jesus upheld and preached continuously till his death, we can discover the three dimensions of this narrow gate, which discipline our lives and make us worthy of walking in right past to our blissful destiny of salvation.

The "narrow gate" is made of our human birth limitations: mainly, every one of us lives with a weak and fragile body. And so did Jesus. But he hugged it, loved it, and did the best he could despite its limitations. Scriptures quote him. *"When he came into the world, he said: 'Sacrifice and offering you did not desire, but a body you prepared for me.' Then I said, 'As is written of me in the scroll, behold, I come to do your will, O God'"* (Heb. 10:5, 7). With Jesus, we are aware of the fact that this earthly body is so limited that, at any time, it can betray us or disown us. It is unpredictable in its cooperation with us but always predictable that it will meet its own disintegration—namely, death. We—though rational beings, only little less than angels—are blindfolded by our ignorance. Our ways are not God's ways. His thoughts are not our thoughts. His way is the High Way. He makes his own choices. Those who are first here will be last there, and those who are last now will be first in heaven. We may try to accomplish all sorts of things here in our own way, but God has his own way of judging them. As Jesus underscores, our judgment about our undertakings and achievements can easily be thwarted by the all-wise God on our Judgment Day.

There is another constituent of the narrow gate. It is the burdensome bundle of our day-to-day sufferings. We come across so many sufferings and pains in every dimension of our lives: physical, mental, emotional, psychological, and spiritual. All of them hurt us very badly. All of us carry for life so many of the scars of such wounds. Why are all these happening to us? The author of the Letter to the Hebrews candidly responds to this question: *"All are permitted by our Father to discipline us. He does this only because he loves us. He does this only to his loved children so that they can be disciplined, pruned, groomed to enter through the narrow gate to heaven."*

The third element of the narrow gate is nothing but the intrusion of others into our lives. To be alone is much better than to be squeezed by others. Both in our family as well as in our community environment, we encounter such troublesome "squeezing" of others in our safe and restful territory. Though it isn't right, we still dream of being let alone as a lonely island. Being a bachelor, I feel a little jealous of married people who are very much blessed to be saved, because they are truly going through the narrow gate as Jesus demands. Added to the family environment, we have to live in a community. We call it neighborhood, town, parish, church, nation, and the international order. There too we have to be intruded on by others—strangers, refugees, migrants, the unwanted, people of different opinions, different colors, different faiths, different values, and so on.

God's eternal dream is for all creation to live together as one family—his sons and daughters. He prophesied his dream through Isaiah: *"I am coming to gather all nations and tongues; they shall come and see my glory"* (Isa. 66:18). As Israelites, we hate it because, many times, it hurts us. God invites everyone to his banquet. Individuality is not the best source of being saved. Unquestionably, a community life is a pain in the neck. To bring everybody together to work with us is so hard, and it is simply a martyrdom to be undergone in common works. We have to—by all means—accept everyone in our life, though it pricks us and hurts us. That is the way to be disciplined to go through the narrow gate.

Jesus is the way, the truth, the life, and the "gate." This is why we have to follow his footsteps; and surely, we will walk his walk through the narrow gate and reach heaven.

FORTIETH WEEKEND

Twenty-Second Sunday of the Year
The Code of Conduct in God's Banquet

"When you are invited by someone to a wedding banquet, do not recline at table in the place of honor. A more distinguished guest than you may have been invited by him, and the host who invited both of you may approach you and say 'Give your place to this man,' and then you would proceed with embarrassment to take the lowest place. Rather, when you are invited, go and take the lowest place so that when the host comes to you, he may say, 'My friend, move up to a higher position.' Then you will enjoy the esteem of your companions at the table. For everyone who exalts himself will be humbled, but the one who humbles himself will be exalted." Then he said to the host who invited him, "When you hold a lunch or a dinner, do not invite your friends or your brothers or your relatives or your wealthy neighbors, in case they may invite you back and you have repayment. Rather, when you hold a banquet, invite the poor, the crippled, the lame, the blind; blessed indeed will you be because of their inability to repay you. For you

> *will be repaid at the resurrection of the*
> *righteous."* (Luke 14:7–14)

Any sophisticated and civilized community gathering demands some codes of conduct like a dress code, table manners, bodily gestures, the tone of voice and restrictions in words uttered, and even the quantity of food ingested. Those who observe such etiquette will be honored highly, given a warm welcome, and offered high places in those gatherings. Most of us base our security on either how we join with elite groups of society or what the world offers us, like riches, possessions, education, titles, good names, and social praises and well-groomed appearances. Almost all of us have succumbed to such bad attitudes. Surprisingly, Jesus recommends this weekend meditation a different base for our security. He proposes a unique etiquette to be observed in the Kingdom of God he has established, as another option for his fellow men. We can call it "the kingdom manners."

First, for the hosts, Jesus promulgates an etiquette of equality. The Kingdom of God is the perfect society in which God's spiritual meals are provided for everyone, not just as a private dinner for two by candlelight. All the dishes on the table are for everyone equally. There is enough and more for every single person's needs. It is an occasion of sharing and joyfulness. Those who act as hosts must not show any discrimination whatsoever in inviting and feeding the guests. Jesus wants them to be polite and kind to their guests—to the strangers as well as their near ones. They should never judge them according to their outward appearances or their backgrounds. All are the same as God's children and friends of Jesus.

As for the guests, Jesus proposes the etiquette of humility. He admonishes the guests to be modest, humble, and simple, and to wait until their hosts take them to the prescribed tables. Humility is plainly and simply the proper understanding of our own worth. It is neither to overestimate one's worth nor to underestimate one's self either, for that would be self-contempt. To feel self-contempt is to feel worthless and to live without any hope for improvement or achievement. Instead, we simply admit the truth about ourselves. We do not know everything; we do not do everything right. We are all imperfect and sinners.

Nevertheless, we also recognize that we are made in the image and likeness of God and that we are called and empowered to help build the Kingdom of God with our God-given gifts. Confirming this truthful fact in God's Kingdom, the Book of Sirach exhorts: *"My son, conduct your affairs with humility, and you will be loved more than a giver of gifts. Humble yourself the more, the greater you are, and you will find mercy in the sight of God"* (Sir. 3:17–18). And in the Gospel, Jesus proclaims: *"For whoever makes himself out to be great will be humbled, and whoever humbles himself will be raised."*

The basic element behind these codes of conduct is the belief that our survival and security in this life depends on our Creator God; and the only status that counts is one's relationship with God. Our real status is measured not by our rank or occupation but by the level of love and service offered to God through our relationships with those around us. This calls for a strong inner security, which is independent of arbitrarily conferred status or position. This inner conviction is generated from the believable fact that we, as Christians, already have come to Mount Zion and the city of the living God, where our position gets stronger and all the fears are smashed (Heb. 12:22).

We are always both guests and hosts in God's banquet of life. We become guests when we share the gifts and blessings of God in everyday life; at the same time, we too turn out to be hosts when, for the sake of God and in Jesus's name, we share the same blessings with our needy brothers and sisters in the family, community, and the entire human family. By applying Jesus's code of etiquette to our life situations, let us be the best hosts and the best guests in his kingdom.

FORTY-FIRST WEEKEND

Twenty-Third Sunday of the Year
Jesus-Oriented Detachment
Enhances All Our Attachments

> *Great crowds were traveling with him, and he turned and addressed them, "If any one comes to me without hating his father and mother, wife and children, brothers and sisters, and even his own life, he cannot be my disciple. Whoever does not carry his own cross and come after me cannot be my disciple . . . In the same way, every one of you who does not renounce all his possessions cannot be my disciple."*
>
> (Luke 14:25–33)

Our life is a bundle of relationships through which we are made what we are. Once we were in the womb of our mother, a lump of mere flesh and bones. But later, as we grew, we became humans, thanks to the connections we established with God and our fellow men. Religions, as any other natural helps, are there to make those relationships stronger, more fruitful, and more successful. And so does our Christianity. In the Gospel passage taken for our meditation this weekend, Jesus demands such terrible and hurting and uncompromising behavior from us who plan to enjoy his new life in our religion. Let us listen again to what he says: *"Unless you turn your back on father or mother, wife or children, brother or sister, and your very selves, you cannot be my followers."* To many of us, these words of Jesus may seem horrible and very hurting in our daily life. But if we go deeper into them in the light of the Spirit, we discover the most useful and fruitful strategy in maintaining our human relationships.

Let us be very clear about one thing. When Jesus arrived on this earth, with a striking note, he taught us how to sustain the remarkable relationship established between God and ourselves, and even among ourselves. First, he claimed and proved himself as God with us, Emmanuel, and demanded from us the same kind of relationship with him to be retained as we uphold with God. This is what his religion is all about. It is a new religion with new life, a new life with a new idea of relationship. In this new relationship with Jesus, we are commanded to be total and wholistic in giving up our very self to his love. Most of the time, we are tempted to be halfhearted and even back off from obeying this command. In our discipleship with him, Jesus doesn't just want a bit of us. He wants all of us. Any love game in life demands a total claim upon the Beloved. Love claims the Beloved, totally. He has given himself totally to us. For our relationship with him to flourish, we have to accept his gift of himself and give ourselves totally to him. The relationship to the Lord demands living his life and even following him in sacrifice. *"You cannot be my follower unless you take up your cross."* A relationship with the Lord means putting him before our possessions. *"You cannot be my disciple unless you renounce all your possessions."*

When Jesus says *"leave your relations and even your very self,"* he does not mean to desert everybody at home and all our friends and become a lonely person or an isolated island in the universe. On the contrary, he expects us to build up all our relationships in this world not by mere natural bases like blood and flesh, human laws, contracts, or racial, creedal, national, regional, tribal, civic, and social foundations, but on the love of Jesus, the justice of God, the morality of innocence, the human dignity of God's child, and the freedom of God's Spirit, peace, forgiveness, and joy of heaven. Any relationship we create in this world as spouses in marriage, parent and child at home, leader and follower in any social and political arena, should not lack this Gospel foundation.

To explain such Gospel-oriented human relationships, there are many events and sayings found in beautiful events described in the letters of Paul. One among them, the shortest (Letter to Philemon), is where Paul writes from prison to his friend, urging him to take back a slave who had apparently done something wrong but who, under Paul's influence, had become a Christian. Paul exhorts him to accept the converted slave, as he relates to the slave as an affectionate father, brother, and even as a part of his self (Phile. 1:9–17). This indicates that in the Kingdom of God Jesus preached, if some of our natural relationships obstruct us to embrace such a "macrofamily spirit" of Jesus, we should even detach them to gain indestructible eternal life. We are born for such a destiny, though we are vulnerable to become the very dust and be annihilated like all other creatures (Ps. 90:3–6). However, there are those of us who adhere to the words of wisdom that came from our Creator, Jesus Christ, about whom the Book of Wisdom prophesied: *"Who can know your counsel, unless you give Wisdom and send your Holy Spirit from on high? Thus were the paths of those on earth made straight, and people learned what pleases you, and were saved by Wisdom"* (Wis. 9:17–18).

FORTY-SECOND WEEKEND

Twenty-Fourth Sunday of the Year
Come, Let Us Destroy First Our
Own Molten Calves

Then the Lord said to Moses: "Go down at once because your people, whom you brought out of the land of Egypt, have acted corruptly. They have quickly turned aside from the way I commanded them, making for themselves a molten calf and bowing down to it, sacrificing to it and crying out, 'These are your gods, Israel, who brought you up from the land of Egypt!' I have seen this people, how stiff-necked they are," continued the Lord to Moses. "Let me alone, then, that my anger may burn against them to consume them. Then I will make of you a great nation." But Moses implored the Lord, his God, saying . . . "Turn from your burning wrath; change your mind about punishing your people . . ." So the Lord changed his mind about the punishment he had threatened to inflict on his people.

(Exod. 32:7–14)

The God whom we worship is a God of love, compassion, forgiveness, goodness, justice, and peace. He is a God of life. As Pope John Paul II said, when God gives life, he creates it for eternity. Indeed, as we meditate this weekend on the marvelous deed of God to his people from the Old Testament, we notice him first being so vexed and disturbed by the people's misbehavior and infidelity. As we hear often, preachers contending God loves the sinners but hates the sins; the "thrice-holy" God can never bear unholiness smeared on his image and likeness, which he had created humans with.

We humans have a tendency to create our own god, as the Israelites had created by their own hands. There are people among us who are slaves to the molten calf of fanaticism, death, violence, hatred, violence, and terrorism. Many others surrender to the molten calf of hatred, retaliation, and vengeance; and so many in the world worship a molten calf of secularism, materialism, licentiousness, worldliness, and immorality. These kinds of worshippers of the molten calf can be found in all present-day life situations: developed and underdeveloped, educated and uneducated, poor and rich, religious and irreligious.

The greatest underlying problem, hidden under the carpet of these man-made devotions, is nothing but the ignorance and arrogance of fake-self dominated humans. That is why God calls them the "stiff-necked generation," and he cries out sternly, "Forty years I loathed that generation; I said: 'This people's heart goes astray; they do not know my ways.' Therefore, I swore in my anger: 'They shall never enter my rest'" (Ps. 95:10–11). Saul, who became Paul, confessed this truth about his past sinful life: *"I was once a blasphemer and a persecutor and an arrogant man, but I have been mercifully treated because I acted out of ignorance in my unbelief"* (1 Tim. 1:13).

Very fortunately, we know the God we worship never keeps his resentment against us. He, rather, is a God who hates sin but loves the sinner. He has shown himself as the Lord of both justice and mercy. So, in the scriptures, we read: *"The Lord changed his mind about the punishment he had threatened to inflict on his people."* And the forgiven Paul testifies: *"I was mercifully treated, so that in me, as the foremost, Christ Jesus might display all his patience as an example for those who would come to believe in him for everlasting life"* (1 Tim. 1:16).

Jesus, coming from his Father, preached a Gospel of mercy and acted it out in life, telling us, "I came to call sinners." If we browse all his sayings in the Gospels, we can notice two-thirds of them proclaim that God of Jesus is eternally merciful. The three parables he narrated about the lost-and-found coin, sheep, and prodigal son cover the central message of his mercy proclamation. He underlines at the end of each story how his Father would be happy when he forgives and accepts the repentant sinners. *"I tell you, there will be more joy in heaven over one sinner who repents than over ninety-nine righteous people who have no need of repentance"* (Luke 15:1–32).

Almost all disciples of Jesus today, together with many religious leaders, shout out the truthful facts of sinful humanity. Many may try to take steps to eradicate the grim situation. But God in Jesus expects us, before waging war against the evil forces outside, to humbly submit to the supremacy of our God of love and fight against the molten calves we ourselves have made or cooperated in making. Let us start to discipline ourselves in accordance with the commandments of the Lord. "The future of the world," as Pope Pius XII said after World War II, "will be in the hands of those who love life."

FORTY-THIRD WEEKEND

*For the children of this world are more
prudent in dealing with their own
generation than are the children of light. I
tell you, make friends for yourselves with
dishonest wealth, so that when it fails, you
will be welcomed into eternal dwellings.
The person who is trustworthy in very
small matters is also trustworthy in great
ones; and the person who is dishonest
in very small matters is also dishonest
in great ones. If, therefore, you are not
trustworthy with dishonest wealth, who
will trust you with true wealth? If you
are not trustworthy with what belongs to
another, who will give you what is yours?
No servant can serve two masters. He will
either hate one and love the other, or be
devoted to one and despise the other. You
cannot serve God and mammon.*

(Luke 16:8–13)

This weekend meditation is all about money. The
naked truth is that no one can survive in this world without
money in any form. Money is a means of bargaining for
our livelihood among one another. It is only a symbol of
what we give and what we get. It is a basic instrument for

any human interaction. Most of the relationships, however intimate they may be, are built on this "money."

Therefore, money is as good as my body. It stands as a symbol of our own identity and worth. We labor and, through the wages, our labor is acknowledged. As Jesus's people, we are not asked to hate this money. When the Lord said "You cannot serve two masters: God and Mammon," he never intended to put a conflict between God and the money. Rather, he pointed out the war to be waged between the Supreme God and the possessor of money. We can derive this conclusion from the manner Jesus treated money and money-owners, or moneylenders, in his life. Money by itself is not the root of all evil. Rather, as the correct translation of the biblical verse *Cupiditas est radix malorum* says: "The love of money is the root of all evil."

The Word of God teaches us how we should handle money with care, both in acquiring and using it as well. Prophets like Amos had been warning, with curses from God, those rich people who acquire wealth by exploiting the innocent, the poor, and the ignorant of the society (Amos 8:4–7). Jesus many times cautioned rich people; sometimes he cursed them for their misusing riches (Luke 18:24). *"Owe to you who are rich, for you have received your consolation"* (Luke 6:24). He too used many parables to teach humans how to use money: the parable of the dishonest steward (Luke 16:1–8), the parable of the rich man and Lazarus (Luke 16:19–30), and the parable of the rich fool (Luke 12:16–21).

On one side, Jesus acquired money provided by his own friends out of their resources (Luke 8:3); and he also carefully used it for different purposes (Matt. 17:24–27). He praised those who used their money, be it even a dime, for good causes and with a cheerful heart: *"But she (widow) from her poverty, has contributed all she had, her whole livelihood"* (Mark 12:41–44). "If you wish to be perfect, go, sell what you have and give to the poor, and you will have treasure in heaven" (Matt. 19:16–30).

From his living style and through his sayings, Jesus wants us to acquire money in a right and just way: by our sweat and blood, by our toil and talents, by our sincere efforts and smartness. At the same time, he demands from us to start using this money in his ways, as his faithful stewards, because he is the giver and owner of all our resources. He advises us to use this money in order to make numerous friends so that they can assist us in reaching our home: heaven. Money should help us not to buy people for our own gratification and self-glory, but for the greater glory of God and for earning our dues in the life to come.

What a wonderful gift of God is money, which can be earned and used for our eternal salvation. As Paul writes, *"This is the only way to lead a quiet and tranquil life in all devotion and dignity; and this is good and pleasing to God, our savior, who wills everyone to be saved and to come to knowledge of the truth"* (1 Tim. 2:2–4).

FORTY-FOURTH WEEKEND

Twenty-Sixth Sunday of the Year
Blessed Are the Poor in Spirit but Rich in Mercy

> *There was a rich man who dressed in purple garments and fine linen and dined sumptuously each day. And lying at his door was a poor man named Lazarus, covered with sores, who would gladly have eaten his fill of the scraps that fell from the rich man's table. Dogs even used to come and lick his sores. When the poor man died, he was carried away by angels to the bosom of Abraham. The rich man also died and was buried, and from the netherworld, where he was in torment, he raised his eyes and saw Abraham far off and Lazarus at his side. And he cried out, "Father Abraham, have pity on me. Send Lazarus to dip the tip of his finger in water and cool my tongue, for I am suffering torment in these flames." Abraham replied, "My child, remember that you received what was good during your lifetime while Lazarus likewise received what was bad; but now he is comforted here, whereas you are tormented . . ."* (Luke 16:19–31)

In the story we take for this weekend meditation, Jesus introduces his two dominant characters with a single note.

About the rich man, he said, "There was a rich man." Jesus did not say "There was a man who made lots of money" or "There was a man who started with nothing and made a fortune." Regarding the second notable character, Jesus presented him saying, "There was a beggar." He did not say that Lazarus lost his money in the market or that he was too lazy to earn a living. This gives us a clue what message our Master intended to convey to us.

His story is not about a particular rich and poor man, but about the general state of being rich or poor. That means, in a biblical way, Jesus divides humanity into two principal categories: the category of *Lazaruses* (in Hebrew, the term means "God is my help") and that of *Diveses* (in Latin, the term indicates the rich man). Biblically, this difference is maintained to stress that God can help and support only the first category of people, who are also called *Anawim*.

Our Teacher invites us to notice how the Diveses behave when they are feeling full. They go to the front of the line and look down on others. They consider themselves better and deserving of respect. They also are certain their rich status would remain forever. Even if they face some loss or failure in maintaining or increasing their wealth, position, and properties, they are confident by their IQ and shrewdness that they can earn them back. With this sort of "rich" attitude of satisfaction, they don't care about depending on others, including the Creator.

They too deal life as a business of buying and selling everybody and everything around them only for their success and self-gratification. Jesus emphasizes that even this "business dealing" attitude continues after their death. According to Jesus's story, while the rich man is burning in hellfire, he makes certain deals and negotiations with

Abraham. He never gives up his pride or hardheadedness or his arrogant self-imposing personality. He behaves the same way as he was used to being listened to and making deals. And when he cannot save himself, he tries to keep the money in the family by using Lazarus as a servant-messenger to warn his brothers. God, with Moses, giggles at his pathetic effort.

On the contrary, the first group of people (Lazaruses, or the poor in spirit) tend always not to have what they want or even what they need, and they therefore tend to depend on others. Especially God, who they esteem is their champion. We hear in the canticle of Mary, who burst out singing the praises of the Almighty Champion who sides forever only with the first category of people but thwarts the malicious attitude and behavior of the second group: *"His mercy is from age to age to those who fear him. He has shown might with his arm, dispersed the arrogant of mind and heart. He has thrown down the rulers from their thrones but lifted up the lowly. The hungry he has filled with good things; the rich he has sent away empty"* (Luke 1:50–53).

That is what Jesus expects us to uphold about God's mighty deals among us. As humans, we are prone to either dream of becoming members of the second social elite club—and if not, to feel jealous of those who have already reached their puffed-up position. And we too dislike being beggars in the hands of God due to our pride and self-prestige. This attitude must be diverted to see the people who are standing behind us as the poorer.

Today, the rich manipulate the poor to become richer; and in the process, the poor become poorer. Pope John Paul II constantly quoted this passage to challenge the rich nations of the world to see the impoverished people, who are often at their doorsteps. The world around us provides us with countless opportunities to change our lives. We seldom make use of these chances. We are overburdened with selfish needs and ends. Though we are unfaithful, God continually pours his grace upon us and calls us to repentance and conversion. For this, we need to live out each moment of our existence as an act of love.

FORTY-FIFTH WEEKEND

Twenty-Seventh Sunday of the Year
We Need Increase in Quality of
Faith, Not in Its Quantity

The apostles said to the Lord, "Increase our faith." The Lord replied, "If you have faith the size of a mustard seed, you would say to [this] mulberry tree, 'Be uprooted and planted in the sea,' and it would obey you. Who among you would say to your servant who has just come in from plowing or tending sheep in the field, 'Come here immediately and take your place at table'? Would he not rather say to him, 'Prepare something for me to eat. Put on your apron and wait on me while I eat and drink. You may eat and drink when I am finished'? Is he grateful to that servant because he did what was commanded? So should it be with you. When you have done all you have been commanded, say, 'We are unprofitable servants; we have done what we were obliged to do.'"

(Luke 17:5–10)

There was a plausible life background behind the request of the Twelve: *"Increase our faith."* We always think the apostles and other disciples experienced crises, persecutions, rejections, and tribulations when they were left alone to preach and teach and witness Jesus's Gospel

162

after he went to heaven; but they faced many problems also during their staying and walking with Jesus while he was alive. They should have been psychologically overwhelmed by Jesus's conditions and demands in following him as his disciples, such as to leave everything, including properties, relationships, and even their very selves, etc.

Those discipleship requirements were too hard to be digested and fulfilled. Hence they needed the virtue of faith. They realized they did not have enough faith to cope with Jesus's Gospel demands. Hence they begged Jesus to "increase their faith." Jesus understood their request.

Luke took this occasion to make Jesus expound clearly the content and power of faith. While the disciples prayed for the quantity of faith to be enlarged, Jesus seemed desiring more for its quality to be enhanced. This is why he answered their appeal by pointing out the mustard-seed kind of faith. *"If you had faith as a grain of mustard seed, you could say to this sycamore tree, 'Be rooted up, and be planted in the sea,' and it would obey you."* He meant the strength of faith does not depend on how big it is, but rather its inner content. In order to explain the latter and how to enlarge the quality of their faith, he used a small parable of the master and his slave.

If we deeply meditate on this parable, we can discover Jesus emphasizing three ingredients of faith that should be developed and nurtured by every disciple. Faith in God must first be approached, not merely as a bundle of creeds to be known, memorized, and recited regularly, but as some enrichment of our inner spirit of trust and confidence that our God is near us, even when he seems so far away. That he will take care of his own.

Secondly, deeper and well-developed faith contains the spirit of total love. In a true love relationship, one does not

163

say, "Well, darling, I have loved you for three hours. Now it is your turn to love me back for three hours." The same is true in our loving relationship with God; genuine joy and satisfaction comes from unconditional giving and sharing.

And thirdly, Jesus underlined that our quality of faith must be enhanced by continuous service to God and our neighbors. Our relationship with God is not about buying and selling, but one of total and unconditional love and service. The very energies with which we serve him are his gift to us. We are "merely servants." We can never do more than "our duty." Our attitude must be that of a humble servant. So Jesus said: "*When you have done all that is commanded you, say, 'We are unworthy servants; we have only done what was our duty.'*"

We all need now more and greater faith than ever before. The main reason is worse than ever before our lives are in very critical situations. Problems, crises, confusions, wars, terrorism, and violence are found in every corner of the world. Some are bad, others worse. Often, in these life-threatening situations, we are reduced to a sense of helplessness and hopelessness. One thing is sure: such problems concerning the survival of human lives are not anything new to humans. It all started at the onset as humanity began to evolve. But there is a vast difference between what humanity faced in olden times and what we do at present. Whereas the tribal man had a restricted outer vision about what was happening around him, the civilized man has got a larger vision of the entire universe. What is happening even in the little corner of Africa or Asia comes into his home and heart and knocks him down. There is an astronomical enlargement of his outer vision of human life due to modern technology and communication.

In those days of tribal life, man managed or coped with the crises of his time with the little inner vision he had as faith. But today's man—having a greater vision of life, an enlarged understanding of what is going on around the entire globe—cannot handle it with the same tribal faith, which is very narrow and small. Today, this is what Jesus invites us to possess: an enlarged inner vision, which God described to Prophet Habakkuk. *"For still the vision awaits its time; it hastens to the end—it will not lie. If it seems slow, wait for it; it will surely come, it will not delay"* (Hab. 2:3–4).

FORTY-SIXTH WEEKEND

Twenty-Eighth Sunday of the Year
Jesus Seeks the Circumcised Hearts of Disciples

> *As Jesus continued his journey to Jerusalem, he traveled through Samaria and Galilee. As he was entering a village, ten lepers met him. They stood at a distance from him and raised their voice, saying, "Jesus, Master! Have pity on us!" And when he saw them, he said, "Go show yourselves to the priests." As they were going, they were cleansed. And one of them, realizing he had been healed, returned, glorifying God in a loud voice; and he fell at the feet of Jesus and thanked him. He was a Samaritan. Jesus said in reply, "Ten were cleansed, were they not? Where are the other nine? Has none but this foreigner returned to give thanks to God?" Then he said to him, "Stand up and go; your faith has saved you."*
> (Luke 17:11–19)

This weekend, let us meditate with Luke on the basic and intrinsic dimension of discipleship—namely, our close connections with Jesus. He explains this fact through the event of the healing of the ten lepers. Usually, the lepers in Palestine were treated as outcasts; therefore, they had to hide and live in dark caves and shelters. In this event, they seem to be bold enough to break that shelter and come out of it to connect themselves to Christ. Secondly, as they came out of their hidden places, they cried out, not "unclean, unclean" (which they were supposed to shout when they appeared in public so that anyone who walks by should run away from them), but they shouted in loud voices, "Jesus, Son of David, have pity on us." Doing such abnormal things, these lepers showed their faith in Jesus's power and, above all, in his compassion.

Indeed, Jesus liked them for their audacious and impudent prayerful gestures. However, he did not heal them immediately. As God's usual deed, he puts their faith to the test. He commands them to go and show themselves to their priests. He wanted them to continue their rituals and other religious and social practices; even they noticed their prayer had not been answered yet. This is what we observe in the healing story of Naaman the leper in the Old Testament (2 Kings 5:14–17). The prophet listens to the prayers of Naaman for healing. Yet not healing him, he orders him to go and sink ten times into the water. Naaman unhesitatingly obeys. And he was healed. It was the same way when the lepers in the Gospel hurried to fulfill the command of Jesus. On their way, they were healed.

Surely, they were overwhelmed with wonder, surprise, and joy. They surely headed along to the temple to show themselves to the priests. Among them, one breached out of their company and started running back to Jesus. The other nine were attentive, maybe, to socialize themselves and enter into the mainstream of society; and therefore, they decided to fulfill the social and religious ritual and not to please Jesus, their healer. They would have surely forgotten the real source of their healing.

This is well expressed by Jesus when he was inquiring about them from the Samaritan leper. "Where are the other nine?" Jesus too praises the grateful gesture of the returned leper. In other words, Jesus expected every one of his disciples who are called and healed by him to be intimately connected to him. There is no doubt he endorses all our external practices and rituals to show and increase our faith in God. But it is not at all sufficient to be a disciple of Jesus. When we plan to become Jesus's disciples, we must go some more miles—namely, we should fully relate ourselves to Jesus as his intimate friend and lover and connect ourselves to him as branches to a vine. This personal love-approach to the Master will push us forward to keep Jesus as our first priority of life.

This will allow us to start everything, proceed in everything, and end everything in him, through him, and with him. Such intimacy with Christ should be the base and core for all that a disciple does in the name of religious and social rituals and practices. As the Samaritan leper did, in every effort we take to perform rituals and charitable practices, we should express our sentiments of love and gratitude to our Master.

The disciples of Jesus must possess a grateful and mellow heart as the Samaritan leper. Let everything flow out of that heart, everything they perform and accomplish both in social and religious life, whether they are targeted at families, communities, and the entire world. Therefore, if we decide to be closely related disciples of Jesus, we make sure all our performances are generated from our "consecrated and circumcised hearts" (2 Tim. 2:8–13) that are always mellow and grateful, like the heart of our Master.

Twenty-Ninth Sunday of the Year
Quality Prayer for Quality Discipleship

> *Then he told them a parable about the necessity for them to pray always without becoming weary. He said, "There was a judge in a certain town who neither feared God nor respected any human being. And a widow in that town used to come to him and say, 'Render a just decision for me against my adversary.' For a long time, the judge was unwilling, but eventually he thought, 'While it is true that I neither fear God nor respect any human being, because this widow keeps bothering me, I shall deliver a just decision for her lest she finally come and strike me.' The Lord said, 'Pay attention to what the dishonest judge says. Will not God then secure the rights of his chosen ones who call out to him day and night? Will he be slow to answer them? I tell you, he will see to it that justice is done for them speedily. But when the Son of Man comes, will he find faith on earth?'"* (Luke 18:1–8)

In our plan of walking with Jesus as his disciples, we are fully aware of our inability to cope with all his demands. Jesus knew it well, and therefore, he offered us a support in our journey of discipleship. That is called prayer, through which he hears the outcry of the poor and the fragile disciples who are longing to stay in his company. We are "praying people." There is no doubt about it; otherwise, we would not be his disciples. Most of us pray not only here but also at various times, occasions, and in various ways. In our prayer time, we usually adore the Lord as our only God; we sometimes spell out to him what kind of God we worship. Whatever name we give him, we want to make sure we are present in front of him. We include in prayer many praises and thanks for his greatness and fidelity and goodness. We express to him our weaknesses and mistakes and ask his forgiveness. In addition, we list out many petitions and intercessions to him.

Some of us seriously take this prayer as our duty or as our daily need. Most of us take this as an extracurricular activity or as an appendix to the main humdrum affairs of earthly life. So many pray before they go to accomplish certain serious and important jobs. Others pray only when bad and evil things occur, such as death, accident, separation, and deception. Due to such anomaly, faking, frustration, and silliness found in the countless uses of prayer, many among us have drifted away from any kind of prayer effort. Also, some of us are feeling desperate that many of our prayer efforts become barren.

But Jesus, this weekend, invites us to listen to him carefully and rethink about our habit of prayer. His point is this: whatever be our aim, style, mode, and kind of prayer, it must possess an important ingredient that is called perseverance if it is to be genuine and resourceful prayer. Through his parable, he wants to show all his disciples that they should pray continually and not lose heart.

Our beloved Apostle Paul defined *perseverance* very succinctly: "Pray unceasingly." If "praying unceasingly" means endlessly reciting prayers on our knees, we are in big trouble. However, if praying unceasingly means living and breathing and walking and interacting and laughing and loving in a constant spirit of prayer, then this is achievable. In this connection, he poses before us a widow as our role model, who gains finally her victory by her impudent attitude and persevering attempts.

Perseverance is the basics for the victory of Jesus's disciples in their process of becoming most worthy disciples. Let us take any saint or any holy person mentioned in the Bible. Their lives would tell us that they could not and did not achieve their aspirations to become worthy disciples till their deaths. But one thing was certain: they were beloved sons and daughters in whom God was well pleased. He was pleased not much on what they had accomplished for Jesus, nor on their "Guinness World Record" of reciting a thousand and one prayers with no interruption. The only reason for God being pleased with them was that they persevered in prayer and action.

In the Bible (Exod. 17:8–13), we have a historical record-breaker in prayer of perseverance. He was Moses, whom God loved very close to his heart. Even though Moses had his miraculous staff in his hands, even though he climbed up the mountain and prayed, the Lord did not answer his request—namely, a victory for the Israelites and defeat to their enemies. Moses never lost heart. He persevered in prayer, lifting up his hands. His style of praying may seem and sound funny and bizarre. Yet God finally granted a historical victory to his people because of Moses's perseverance in prayer.

Victory, defeat, failure, success—all these are part of human life. Prayer is not something that interferes with the plan of God and changes God and his will. Rather, our prayer of perseverance indicates that our hearts are melted, open for God's grace, and ready to cope with whatever his will has designed for us. Let us remember what Jesus says today at the end of the Gospel: "When the Son of Man comes, will he find faith on earth?"

Thirtieth Sunday of the Year
In God's Kingdom, Power Comes Only by Humility

He then addressed this parable to those who were convinced of their own righteousness and despised everyone else. "Two people went up to the temple area to pray; one was a Pharisee and the other was a tax collector. The Pharisee took up his position and spoke this prayer to himself, 'O God, I thank you that I am not like the rest of humanity—greedy, dishonest, adulterous—or even like this tax collector. I fast twice a week, and I pay tithes on my whole income.' But the tax collector stood off at a distance and would not even raise his eyes to heaven but beat his breast and prayed, 'O God, be merciful to me a sinner.' I tell you, the latter went home justified, not the former; for everyone who exalts himself will be humbled, and the one who humbles himself will be exalted." (Luke 18:9–14)

Throughout the scriptures, we come across thousands of references to highlight the importance of humbling ourselves to our Creator. Though he allows us to call him "Abba, Father," and though he calls us spouse, we cannot deny his holiness and greatness and certainly our own fragile creatureliness. Besides, we are encouraged by God's deeds toward the humble, meek, poor, and sinful humans. He acts as their "champion." Jesus emphasized such a consoling Gospel message to the downtrodden.

In the parable we have taken for this weekend meditation, Jesus brings to our attention two symbolic characters that represent two groups of our society. The group of sinful but contrite people are exemplified by the tax collector who suffered from the loneliness caused by his sins. He had many things in life. He was rich. But he was alone. He had no friends other than other tax collectors, people as despicable as he was. His people hated him. His family hated him. He hated himself. Surely, God must hate him. So he slipped into the temple and sincerely sought God's forgiveness, and God heard the cries of this abandoned one.

On the other side, we notice the Pharisee, an epitome of the self-righteous men and women. He clearly has evidence to prove that he is the "good" person. He carefully keeps the Law of the Jews and the commandments of God. He faithfully observes the obligations of a good Jew: he prays, he fasts, and he gives alms. And yet, according to Jesus, God is not happy with him because, basically, he is a totally self-centered person. What he really says to God is "God, you should be deeply grateful that you have someone like me, someone who is so faithful in following your commands . . ."

Jesus never ceased to proclaim that his Father is eternally a friend and champion of the needy and sinners. In the Book of Sirach, we read: *"God will not disadvantage the poor, he who hears the prayer of the oppressed. He does not disdain the plea of the orphan, nor the complaint of the widow. The one who serves God wholeheartedly will be heard; his petition will reach the clouds. The prayer of the humble person pierces the clouds, and he is not consoled until he has been heard."* Here we should remember God always loves the sinner but not the sins. And we should be well aware of the kind of sinner he likes, and the kind of poor he listens to. God becomes champion only of the sinners who accept truthfully their sinful status. When they begin to humble themselves in front of God sincerely, their cry is surely being heard by the Creator. This is what Jesus proclaimed: *"For whoever makes himself out to be great will be humbled, and whoever humbles himself will be raised."*

Humans with humility are always pleasing God in whatever situation they are in. Humility is plainly and simply nothing but the proper understanding of our own worth. Humble persons never overestimate their worth. However, it does not presuppose that they need to underestimate their self-worth either, for that would be self-contempt. To have humility is to be true to oneself. Those who are truly humble believe themselves to have nothing when, in fact, they have everything because they possess God. In a word, those who humble themselves, God justifies! Humility is not denying the truth but affirming it without pride and self-assertiveness, as Paul alleges loudly, "I have fought the good fight. I have finished the race, I have kept the faith" (2 Tim. 4:6−8).

One of the rare virtues we do not find today in the world is humility. This may be because our forebears misinterpreted it as against self-esteem. We are told again and again to be proud of ourselves, our culture, our nation, and our racial backgrounds. And thus, we keep our self-esteem boosted. The vice of pride takes dominant role in every step of our lives. Unfortunately, we lost the beautiful virtue of humility, especially in our relations with God. So many blessings therefore turn out to be curses to our children and the nations. We hear a popular song has been played repeatedly on the radio. It is Lee Greenwood's "Proud to be an American." It's a nice song. But one of the spiritual authors thinks that it would be a little better if Lee Greenwood altered the words of the chorus to be "I'm *blessed* to be an American."

FORTY-NINTH WEEKEND

Thirty-First Sunday of the Year
Humans, Created Good, but
Saved to Become Better

"Now a man there named Zacchaeus, who was a chief tax collector and also a wealthy man, was seeking to see who Jesus was; but he could not see him because of the crowd, for he was short in stature. So he ran ahead and climbed a sycamore tree in order to see Jesus, who was about to pass that way. When he reached the place, Jesus looked up and said to him, "Zacchaeus, come down quickly, for today I must stay at your house." And he came down quickly and received him with joy . . . Zacchaeus stood there and said to the Lord, "Behold, half of my possessions, Lord, I shall give to the poor, and if I have extorted anything from anyone, I shall repay it four times over." And Jesus said to him, "Today salvation has come to this house . . . For the Son of Man has come to seek and to save what was lost." (Luke 19:1–10)

Our scriptures and tradition never become tired of proclaiming to humanity for centuries that our God in Jesus relates himself to any sinner on earth. *"He is merciful to all, he does overlook men's sins that they may repent.*

He loves them because his immortal spirit is in all of them. Therefore he corrects, little by little, those who trespass, and reminds and warns them of the things wherein they sin, that they may be freed from wickedness and put their trust in him" (Wis. 12:1). The Psalmist, several times, repeats his favorite litany: *"The Lord is kind and full of compassion, slow to anger, abounding in love"* (Ps. 144). The one and only message that Jesus lived and preached—and for which he established his church—is the same one of God's mercy his forebears experienced.

In the Gospel passage we meditate on this weekend, Luke brings home to us not only Jesus's good news of mercy, but also the gimmicks we play with God and the games played by him too. Zacchaeus was a public sinner. He was a dishonest person at his job of tax-collecting. People looked on him with contempt, mainly because in their eyes, he was a traitor to his religious and national heritage. The unanimous verdict by the public on Zacchaeus was "guilty!"

Inevitably, a rich man like Zacchaeus would have been privately disturbed about his dishonest life—in which case he was intimidated to appear in the crowd, as he wanted to be acquainted with Jesus. This is why he climbed up the tree to look for him. This is the typical behavior of any sinner. When we commit any sin against God and others, we try to hide out from the public, sometimes like our first parents did (Gen. 3:8). We try to hide ourselves from God by becoming very busy in our development. Many of us use put-on smiles or behave as champions of safeguarding morality or joining in any one of the extreme positions and ideologies like terrorism, fanaticism, and fundamentalism and so on. This is what Zacchaeus did in the Gospel event.

However, while most of us, in order to appease our guilty conscience, make recourse to drug addiction, alcoholism, or any other perversions, Zacchaeus was searching for Jesus and his acquaintance for getting relief. According to Luke, there exists perennially a high "psychic vibration" between Jesus and his disciples, whom he would be recruiting for his cause. Immediately finding the contrite heartbeat of the sinful "would-be disciple," he looked up and said to him, *"Zacchaeus! Make haste and come down; for I must stay at your house today."*

That is the heart of Jesus. Jesus pardoned Zacchaeus's sins not just because he offered him a sumptuous dinner. As the Gospel says, the sinner showed his repentance by the loving gesture of penitential reparation in front of the public. He decided to share most of his riches with the poor and with those he hurt by his injustice as retribution. This made Jesus say, *"Today salvation has come to this house, since he also is a son of Abraham."*

Come, let us do something about our burden of guilt, which is bothering us, with positive steps, as taken by Zacchaeus, to liberate ourselves from guilt feelings. The Creator made us humans out of clay in order to be good, in the sense to be godly and live and enjoy God's favor and peace. But like Zacchaeus, many times we fail to be so and fall into the pit of desolation. But out of his mercy, God sent his Son, Jesus, through whom we are given salvation to become "better" and "greater" as our Creator intended.

FIFTIETH WEEKEND

Thirty-Second Sunday of the Year
Our God Is Not God of the Dead but of the Living

> *Jesus said to them, "The children of this age marry and are given in marriage; but those who are deemed worthy to attain to the coming age and to the resurrection of the dead neither marry nor are given in marriage. They can no longer die, for they are like angels; and they are the children of God because they are the ones who will rise. That the dead will rise even Moses made known in the passage about the bush, when he called 'Lord' the God of Abraham, the God of Isaac, and the God of Jacob; and he is not God of the dead, but of the living, for to him all are alive."*
>
> (Luke 20:27–38)

Every one of us longs to live a life of peace, joy, freedom, peace, and justice. Whenever we do not possess today such a fulfilling life, we wish for "a better tomorrow, a better future, a better life." This desire and dream is innate in our nature because we know we have been created by a God who is life. When Moses asked God what was his name, God replied, "I am Who I Am," which is what Jesus quotes in the Gospel passage taken for our meditation. Our God is a living God enjoying fullness of life. Being his creatures, naturally, we are inclined to possess such life too. If we don't get it or lose it, we are disappointed, confused, and tense. To add to this struggle, the human death comes in between to worsen our problem.

In this precarious life, the Spirit of Jesus exhorts us not to be afraid of facing death because we would be resurrected surely from death. Death has a very short duration. It is only a means and not an end in itself. Final resurrection as the goal of all living is a central concept of our Christian faith. It is very much a matter of faith and trust in God's Word as we have no proof or prior experience of such a life, nor can we say very much about it. Paul puts it well when he says that *"Eye has not seen nor ear heard all that God has prepared for those who love him."*

We have often been influenced by the images in the Book of Revelation, which has led us to describe heaven as a place where we kneel on clouds, play harps, and sing the praises of God all day long and every day forever. In explaining the life after our death, Jesus contends: *"Those who are resurrected from the dead cannot die anymore, because they are equal to angels and are the sons of God, being sons of the resurrection."* Though there are too many explanations and religious dogmas around this world, we adhere firmly to what Jesus is holding on this issue. We will enjoy a fuller life, a better life than anything we dreamt of but totally different from what has been touched and explained with our limited human brain.

There is no problem in longing and dreaming of a better future and a better life. The real issue is what kind of means we would use to attain that "better tomorrow." In scriptures, we find God handing out to us the means to achieve such a better life through many events and examples. One of them is the life and death of the Maccabees (narrated in 2 Macc. 7:1–14). Up to the end of earthly life, the entire family strived to fulfill all God's laws. *"They indeed kept their feet firmly in God's paths; there was no faltering in their steps"* (Ps. 17:5). Even in the critical moment of their lives, they never deviated themselves from their adherence to their God and his demands. As they were tortured and bleeding to death, they shouted, *"We are ready to die rather than transgress the laws of our fathers."* They burst out, *"You dismiss us from this present life, but the King of the universe will raise us up to an everlasting renewal of life, because we have died for his laws."* They unflinchingly exclaimed, *"I got these from Heaven, and because of his laws, I disdain them, and from him I hope to get them back again."*

We need not wait for such religious wars or persecution, as in the time of Maccabees, to show our steadfastness to God. We, the committed disciples of Jesus, are already martyrs by the existing social order, social upheavals, social injustice, and other problems. Our human life is stifled, disintegrated, disabled, and chronically vulnerable to sickness because of the ignorance, carelessness, and sinfulness of our own parents or grandparents. We undergo self-immolation caused by others' selfishness and hardheadedness. We are caught up in a self-imprisoned life situation due to natural and artificial causes. We need to pass through this valley of darkness and tears with steadfast faith-holding and in adhering very firmly to God's love and service. This is the only way to reach our "better life" after death.

FIFTY-FIRST WEEKEND

Thirty-Third Sunday of the Year
The End Is Horrible, but Its Goal Is Gorgeous

> *For the day is coming, blazing like an oven, when all the arrogant and all evildoers will be stubble. And the day that is coming will set them on fire, leaving them neither root nor branch, says the Lord of hosts. But for you who fear my name, the sun of justice will arise with healing in its wings.* (Mal. 3:19–20)

Wild dreams of today are the practical deeds and enterprises of tomorrow. All of us have dreamed so many wild dreams about our lives in our childhood. And that is what we experience and express and live in today. Only our dreams made us make beautiful choices for life. We have grown, developed, and achieved because of our dreams. Customarily, all religions are based on certain stories and dreams. Christianity is not exempted. Our God always invites us to dream dreams and live through them. We Christians live on wild dreams about God, about life after death. All our dreams are enlisted in our creeds and dogmas. At the end of our regular creed, we recite the most admirable, though unknown, dream of our life's ultimate end: *"He will come again in glory to judge the living and the dead, and his kingdom will have no end. We look for the resurrection of the dead, and the life of the world to come."*

These are indeed wild dreams about our future. Though such dreams may sound weird, we are convinced of their authenticity because of their basis resting on the wild but reality-based dreams of Jesus and the prophets. Jesus's prophecies and predictions about these ultimate things are his wild dreams about human life and the entirety of creation. Along with his forebears, like Prophet Malachi, Jesus spells out very vividly his own version about our final end, which he calls the "Great Day," the "Final Day," a "Day of Judgment," and a "Day of Wrath."

In these biblical versions about the ultimate moment of the universe, certainly the first part of it is about the horrible and stunning disasters and perils. Generally, preachers love to name this event as the "Rapture." Unfortunately, many stop with treating only the first portion of the prophecies in order to frighten their hearers. God has another goal for such description of the end-times. We can observe in every prophecy uttered on this ultimate thing, there is a specific and vivid note about a positive and hope-filled message that is given. At the end of Malachi's prophecy, we read: *"But for you who fear my name, the sun of justice will arise with healing in its wings."*

And in Jesus's exposition of this, the Great Day, we get a positive stroke from him (Luke 21:5–19). First, he advises us not to be fretting over or tossed around by cheaters: *"See that you not be deceived, for many will come in my name, saying, 'I am he,' and 'The time has come.' Do not follow them!"* Then he adds an encouraging word: *"When you hear of wars and insurrections, do not be terrified."* He too promises that during those terrible days, he would bestow his power to do what is right and to testify to him properly. Above all, at the close of his description about the end, he includes emphasizing our responsibility of persevering in him, with him, and for him. *"By your perseverance, you will secure your lives."*

As a matter of fact, all spiritual writers claim that these prophetic wild dreams are perfectly necessary for us to go through this valley of tears. In their view, which we can surely agree with, these dreams make our lives meaningful and our burdens of today light and sweet. They are not at all nightmares. They are the source of strength and guidance for our making proper decisions in daily life. When we see and experience these wild dreams coming true—maybe partially in day-to-day life—we should stand erect, raise our heads, and be alert not only for the external attack of the Evil One but much more our internal demoniac violence.

These dreams and realities, if they are not connected with Jesus's dreams, many times turn to be dangerous to ourselves and to society. They too will stifle our efforts of good works and services as Paul, in his time, noticed among the Thessalonians (2 Thess. 3:7–12). Other times, these dreams take us off the ground, frighten us, and make us feel hopeless, ending in depression and keeping eating and drinking as the only goal in life.

Let us keep up our dreaming wild dreams. Human dreams come out of learning the dreams of others through stories. We should allow ourselves to dream the most meaningful dreams of Jesus. Those are as follows: *"There will be a new heaven and a new earth," "There will be one flock and one shepherd," and "That they all may be one as you and I are one."* Also, let us get the help of God in Jesus to realize all our dreams, however wild they may be. But those dreams must be in accordance with his own dreams about his reign. So let us dream the wild dreams of Jesus about that Day of Wrath, that Day of Judgment, and that

Day of Victory. Anytime, that day will be ours. Besides such far-distance reality of creation's end, Jesus also dreamt about us who are still crawling and groping in the dark. Let us start marching on in his "dreamland of fullness."

FIFTY-SECOND WEEKEND

Feast of Christ the King
Let Us Lead Others Staying Put
to the Throne of the Cross

The people stood by and watched; the rulers, meanwhile, sneered at him and said, "He saved others, let him save himself if he is the chosen one, the Messiah of God." Even the soldiers jeered at him. As they approached to offer him wine, they called out, "If you are King of the Jews, save yourself." Above him, there was an inscription that read, "This is the King of the Jews." Now one of the criminals hanging there reviled Jesus, saying, "Are you not the Messiah? Save yourself and us." The other, however, rebuking him, said in reply, "Have you no fear of God, for you are subject to the same condemnation? And indeed, we have been condemned justly, for the sentence we received corresponds to our crimes, but this man has done nothing criminal." Then he said, "Jesus, remember me when you come into your kingdom." He replied to him, "Amen, I say to you, today you will be with me in Paradise." (Luke 23:35–43)

Usually, a leader of a nation or community emerges from the people—sometimes elected and chosen by people, but always for the people. We can observe this in both the past and present history of humanity. In scriptures, we read the authors of the books add one more thing to "from, by, and for the people"—namely, every step of the making of a leader, if he or she is genuine, includes God's hands upon him or her. For example, in the election of David as king of Israel, we are told God was there in the human process as they crowned him king because he was of their own flesh and blood, because he proved his worth by his chivalrous deeds, and because they were certain that their Lord had anointed him and abided with him (2 Sam. 5:1–3).

In the same track, followers of Jesus accepted him as their leader and king because, surely, he was of their flesh and blood, a person of the human crowd; because he did show his worth and power in their midst; with miraculous deeds; and because they were certain that he had been anointed by God.

Yet the wonder of wonders is while the whole universe—including the Father in heaven—recognized his worth and identity, Jesus never claimed himself as a king. In his lifetime, people tried to make him king, but he denied it and disappeared from their midst. To the wonder-struck people like us, he denied ruthlessly those three elements that we esteem as yardsticks to make somebody a king, do not make him king at all. Rather, he had his own way of making himself a king and leader. He became winner, victor, and ever-conquering king not as our human leaders, kings, and queens did and do. "My kingdom is not of this world," he said.

His deliberation has been demonstrated while he was hanging on the cross. We see a man being executed in shame and ignominy, bleeding and battered on a cross, one of the cruelest and degrading punishments ever devised. Over his head are the mocking words: "This is the King of the Jews." Jesus preferred such a throne of the cross and the crown of thorns than be called a king. It is a place of execution for the very worst of criminals. He hangs shamefully in his nakedness. No disciples are to be seen. Luke mentions no friends, not even women, at the foot of the cross. His only companions are two robbers, also crucified, and a jeering crowd. "If you are the king of the Jews, save yourself!" It is not exactly what we imagine about him. We rather prefer those triumphant pictures where Jesus wears a crown and an expensively embroidered cloak with a scepter. And yet here precisely Jesus is at his most kingly. In the light of his background starting from heaven to Calvary, and of his sayings, we can conclude his concept of becoming a king or queen or any sort of leader to rule and guide others includes these things:

> Emptying oneself; being born poor; relating oneself as a friend to the poor, downtrodden, the sick, the needy, and surely, the sinful; vested strong willpower to defeat the evil of sufferings be traveling into them; by scoring the highest mark in forgiving his enemies; leading a role-model life with no flinching in witnessing truth, nothing but the truth; and above all in breathing, eating, walking, relating, praying, and in anything he did, he was occupied with one and only concern of bringing salvific renewal to the hearts of the humans, his brothers and sisters.

This is the same attitude Jesus wants all of us to uphold in our discipleship with him. We should fully believe that we are not merely subjects of his Kingdom and our King.

We are also his partners in the making, in the bringing about of his Kingdom. We are reminded by Paul that, while Jesus is the head, we are his body. We should be kings and queens because we are his people, kith and kin; because we are chosen and anointed by him; the only thing left to our ability is to prove our worth to be victorious kings and queens in his kingdom. That is possible not by our wealth, IQ, glamour, power, and other human abilities—but only by following Jesus's footsteps of living a humble and simple life and always being very rich in merciful deeds.

Printed in the United States
By Bookmasters